A Quarter Century of Macon County Crime (1960-1984)

By
CL Gammon

LAFAYETTE, TENNESSEE
deepreadpress@gmail.com

Copyright © 2024 by CL Gammon

All Rights Reserved.

The publisher prohibits reproduction, scanning, or distribution of this book in any printed or electronic form without written permission, except for brief passages quoted as part of a literary review.

Please do not take part in or encourage piracy of copyrighted materials in violation of the author's rights. Purchase only authorized editions.

The publisher does not control and does not assume any responsibility for the author's or any third-party websites or their content. Views expressed here are those of the author alone.

First Deep Read Press Edition.

Edited by: Kim Gammon

Cover Design by: Kim Gammon

ISBN: 978-1-954989-65-8

Published by:
DEEP READ PRESS
Lafayette, Tennessee
www.deepreadpress.com
deepreadpress@gmail.com

For Billy Jones, who inspired this book.

Other Local History Titles by CL Gammon

You can find all the local history titles listed below at Amazon or at the Deep Read Press website.

Ballyhoo: John Butler and the Monkey Trial

Bizarre Murders in Tennessee: 13 True Stories

Blood on the Cumberland: The Battle of Hartsville

Death on the Highland: Spanish Flu in Macon County

Dixie Witches: 9 True Southern Witch Trials

Hanging the Macon County Witch

Highland Rim Warriors: Macon County Tennessee and World War II

Murder, Mayhem, and Moonshine: True Macon County Crime Stories

Revenue Raiders: Macon County's Whiskey War

Shallow Graves and Shattered Dreams: Solving the Murders of Three Macon County Men

The Fountain of Youth at Red Boiling Springs, Tennessee, Part 1

The Fountain of Youth at Red Boiling Springs, Tennessee, Part 2

The Macon County Race War

Tiger Strong! Macon County Football, 2024

Contents

1960-1961	pp. 9-10
Etheridge Sentenced.	p. 9
A Case of Embezzlement.	p. 9
Woman Turns Herself In.	p. 10
1962-1963	pp. 11-16
Five Charged in Explosion Case.	p. 11
Two Found Guilty of Manslaughter.	p. 11
Kentuckian Found Not Guilty.	p. 12
Family of Five Murdered.	p. 13
Strange Murder/Suicide	p. 14
One Killed, One Wounded.	p. 15
1964-1965	pp. 17-19
Payoffs and Kickbacks.	p. 17
Drowning After Prison Break.	p. 18
1966-1967	pp. 20-48
A Woman Shoots Her Husband.	p. 20
A Story of Sex Tapes and Blackmail.	p. 21
A Scam?	p. 44
Youth Protesters.	p. 45
Milk Wars.	P. 46
1968-1969	pp. 49-59
Little Boy Set Free.	p. 49
Fugitive Arrested.	p. 53
Stabbed to Death.	p. 54
Macon Man Indicted.	p. 54
A Possible Investigation.	p. 55
A Stolen Car Ring.	p. 57

A Civil Rights Violation?	p. 58
1970-1971	pp. 60-63
"Rowdy" Killed.	p. 60
ATF Gets Rid of Gun.	p. 61
Another Senseless Shooting.	p. 61
A Prison Break.	p. 62
Whiskey Raids.	p. 63
1972-1973	pp. 64-67
Another Slaying.	p. 64
School Board Lawsuit.	p. 65
Man Shot to Death.	p. 65
Governor Offers Reward.	p. 66
A Shooting Near the Public Square.	p. 66
1974-1975	pp. 68-73
A Failed Appeal.	p. 68
Lady Bank Robbers.	p. 68
Tobacco Thieves.	p. 70
Missing Money.	p. 70
Fireman Charged with Arson.	p. 71
A Sunshine Law Violation?	p. 72
1976-1977	pp. 74-77
Hiding a Sports Car.	p. 74
An Entire Family Killed.	p. 74
A Big Pot Bust.	p. 75
A Conflict of Interest?	p. 76
Executives Indicted.	p. 77
1978-1979	pp. 78-83
A Hit and Run Death.	p. 78
A Liquor Store Robbery.	p. 78
Big Drug Round Up.	p. 79
A True Mystery.	p. 81
Fix the Jail or Shut it Down.	p. 82
1980-1981	pp. 84-90
Polluter Fined.	p. 84
A Christmas Eve Murder.	p. 85
Blanton Bid-Rigging.	p. 86

Sexual Misconduct.	p. 88
Sears Driver's Theft.	p. 89
1982-1984	pp. 91-102
Election Contests.	p. 91
No Macon Bridge for Trousdale.	p. 92
County Official Accused of Fraud.	p. 93
Honeymooner Sent to Jail.	p. 94
A Case of Special Treatment?	p. 95
A Woman Sues a Drug Company.	p. 96
A Case of Vehicular Homicide.	p. 97
A Man Sues an Automaker.	p. 99
A Foiled Murder Plot.	p. 100
Macon Sheriff Resigns.	p. 101
Afterword	p. 103
About the Author	p. 104

Introduction

This book takes a look at some of the crimes in Macon County, Tennessee between 1960 and 1984. Most of these short articles deal with what we usually classify as crimes – murder, blackmail, theft, and the like.

But the reader should be aware that some of the stories deal with "crimes" in a broader sense of the word. They include some of the times when people fought to improve the responsiveness of government and some of the times when injured people sought recompence from corporations.

All of these stories are accompanied with sources so that readers can research his own research.

1960-1961

Etheridge Sentenced.

Federal Judge William E. Miller ruled in several cases on March 16, 1960. In one case, Heady D. Etheridge of Lafayette entered a guilty plea to the charges that he had committed forgery with stolen checks. Judge Miller sentenced Etheridge to 30 days in jail.

Source:
Kenyon, Nellie. "Delay Barred in Hatch Case." *The Nashville Tennessean*, March 17, 1960.

A Case of Embezzlement.

U.S. District Judge William E. Miller had a heavy docket of cases to work through when he gaveled in the start of his new session on May 2, 1960. One case that didn't take too long involved two former bank employees from Macon County.

William Pleasant Meador was accused of a decade-long embezzling scheme. Prosecutors presented the judge with evidence that Meador took $48,615.16 from Citizen's Bank in Lafayette between December 1949 and June 20, 1958, while Meador worked at the bank.

Another former employee of the bank, Harold Douglas Williams, was charged aiding in the embezzlement. It was not established exactly how much, if any, of the stolen money went to Williams.

On May 3, both Meador and Williams entered guilty pleas in hopes of getting lighter sentences than they otherwise would have gotten.

Sources:

"2 Plead Guilty to Embezzling." *The Nashville Tennessean*, May 14, 1960.

Woman Turns Herself In.

Celina June Wilburn was a 21-year-old divorcee who had four small children. On January 21, 1961, she turned herself in to the police in Memphis and admitted embezzling $5,717.

Wilburn was born in Macon County, but she had relocated to Memphis and gotten a job working as a bookkeeper for two companies. She was fired on December 30, 1960, when discrepancies in the accounts of both companies were discovered. Wilburn came home to Lafayette, but when she learned warrants had been filed against her, she returned to Memphis to face her punishment. She was charged with three counts of forgery and two counts of grand larceny and went to jail.

Source:

"Young Memphis Mom Held in Embezzlement." *The Nashville Tennessean*, January 18, 1961.

1962-1963

Five Charged in Explosion Case.

On February 17, 1962, five Macon County residents were bound over to a Macon County grand jury charged with "malicious and willful shooting of explosives." Three of the five were juveniles. All five were released after each put up a $1,000 bond. Charged in the case were Paul Stafford, age 22; Charles Porter, age 20; Dewey Swindle, age 17; Garry Goodman, age 16; and Hazel E. Goodman, age 16.

Jim H. Bonham, Deputy State Fire Marshal, investigated the case in conjunction with the Macon County Sheriff's Department. Bonham said the accused had exploded dynamite in a field about a mile and a half northwest of Lafayette. No one was injured, but the explosion broke windows and shook homes over a radius of several hundred yards.

Macon County Sheriff Hubert Knight said four of the five accused had already confessed to their part in setting of the explosion. He said they told him they did it because they want to "have fun and hear the noise."

Source:

"5 Bond Over in Macon Blast." *The Nashville Tennessean*, February 19, 1962.

Two Found Guilty of Manslaughter.

On the evening of March 14, 1962, after deliberation, a Circuit Court jury in Gallatin found Macon County residents Fred Smalling and Victor Flippin. guilty of involuntary manslaughter.

The victim was Kevin Evitts, a seven-year-old Sumner County boy.

The facts, as presented to the jury were that on September 22, 1961, the Evitts boy was riding in a car with his mother and they were traveling in a station wagon along Highway 31-E about four miles west of Gallatin. Suddenly, a car driven by Smalling struck the station wagon in the rear. The impact knocked the Evitts car off the highway. The station wagon knocked over a power pole as it careened into Old Hickory Lake.

Evitts was able to get out of the car, but as he tried to swim to safety, he came too near the high voltage line that was connected to the felled pole, and he was electrocuted.

Smalling drove away from the scene without stopping. But tests by the FBI lab proved that paint on the back of the station wagon matched Smalling's car.

Smalling did not testify, but Flippin, who was Smalling's passenger, did. Flippin said he and Smalling were going to Nashville on the afternoon of September 22. He said that Smalling "tipped" what he thought was a black, two-door sedan near the lake. Flippin continued that they thought the tipping incident was minor and they didn't know Smalling had caused a wreck. That is why, according to Flippin, they didn't stop.

Smalling was handed a sentence of five years in the state prison and Flippin was ordered to serve eleven months and twenty-nine days in the Sumner County jail.

Source:

Raines, Lee. "2 Found Guilty In Boy's Death." *The Nashville Tennessean*, March 25, 1962.

Kentuckian Found Not Guilty.

On March 21, 1962, a criminal court jury in Lafayette acquitted Alton E. Boyles of Tompkinsville, Kentucky of murder charges.

Boyles was charged in the stabbing death of Carlene Short, age 30. The killing allegedly took place about a year earlier. Short was from Macon County, but he had moved to Louisville sometime before.

The prosecution attempted to prove that Boyles stabbed Short to death during a brawl at a dance in Red Boiling Springs. Boyles swore that he didn't stab Short or that they even fought at the dance. The jury believed Boyles and acquitted him.

Source:

"Kentuckian Cleared of Murder Charge." *The Nashville Tennessean*, March 22, 1962.

Family of Five Murdered.

At 5:28 a.m. on April 26, 1962, Nashville firemen answered a call. The residence they entered was ablaze, but what they found inside was worse than a fire. The firemen discovered the bodies of Dewey York, age 38; his wife Velma, age 38; their children, Benny, age 14, and Don, age 4; and Dewey's mother, Lettie, age 71.

Dewey York was from Macon County, but he had moved with his family to Nashville where he sold insurance.

At first, the firemen thought the victims had died from smoke inhalation, but after the blaze was put out, it was determined that they were murder victims. All five had been shot, by a .38-caliber pistol owned by Dewey, and three of them had been stabbed:

Dewey was shot in the chest and was stabbed.
Don was shot in the back and chest, and he was stabbed.
Lettie was shot in the back and she was stabbed.
Velma was shot in the chest.
Bennie was shot in the back.

All the victims were dressed for bed except for Bennie. He was found on the living room floor.

The Davidson County Fire Marshall believed the fire was set to cover up the murders and he surmised the motive for the slaying was robbery. However, two wallets found outside the house belonging to Dewey held a total of $150. It is unknown whether the wallets were taken outside by the firemen; if they were dropped or thrown down by the murderers; or if they were outside for another reason.

The murders of Dewey York and his family were never solved.

Source:

"Investigation Of Slaying Of Former Macon County Family Continues." *The Macon County Times*, May 3, 1962.

Strange Murder/Suicide.

Elsie November *White* Adams, age 49, babysat three of her grandchildren in Nashville during the week, then returned home to Hartsville each weekend. On Thursday March 28, 1963, she was murdered.

Early on the morning of March 28, former Macon County bus driver, Earl Barber, age 55, went to the Nashville home of William Adams, the son of Elsie. Barber asked the Adams man to drive him to where Elsie was babysitting. Since Barber was a family friend, Adams drove him there and waited in the car while Barber went inside.

According to the police, once he was inside the house, Barber pulled a .32-caliber revolver and shot Elsie once in the head, killing her. He then turned the gun on himself and committed suicide by putting a bullet to the head. The three children Elsie was babysitting witnessed the horrific event.

When Barber didn't come out of the house, William Adams became concerned for the first time. It was about 8 a.m. when

Adams entered the house and found the gruesome remains of the two people.

The police couldn't establish a solid motive for the murder-suicide.

Earl Barber is buried at Macon County's Drury Cemetery. The final resting place of Elsie Adams is Macon County's Poney McDonald Cemetery.

Source:

"Dual Slaying Puzzles Police." *The Nashville Tennessean*, March 29, 1963.

One Killed, One Wounded.

On May 6, 1963, a shooting in Nashville left one Macon County man dead, and another critically wounded. Dead was 21-year-old Jimmy H. Steen. Steen was a soldier home on 15-day leave from his duty station at Fort Belvoir, Virginia. The severely wounded man was Ferrel Gammon, age 21, also of Lafayette.

The Nashville police identified Herman Parker, age 24, as the shooter.

Parker's sister-in-law, Betty Burns lived in a house trailer just off Dickerson Road. She told the Nashville police that her sister Mary Ann Parker went there after an argument with Parker, who was her husband. Mary Ann was from Lafayette. Steen and Gammon evidently came to the trailer to visit her.

Betty Burns said, "When I got off work and came home and saw their (Steen and Gammon) car, I was afraid so I went and got Herman. They said they came to see Mary Ann and they argued (with Herman Parker). Herman tried to run them off. He said, 'I've got a gun, and you all better get out of this house.' Jimmy kept telling him to shoot him if he had a gun.

"I went into the back with Mary Ann, and I heard three or four shots. I ran back into the front of the trailer. Jimmy was lying there. He looked up at me and said, 'Betty, I'm dying.'"

Source.

"1 Killed, 1 Hurt in Shooting." *The Nashville Tennessean*, May 7, 1963.

1964-1965

Payoffs and Kickbacks.

On June 26, 1965, a trial was underway in Nashville that had far reaching ramifications. There were allegations that members of the trucking industry had paid cash to get favorable legislation in Kentucky and Tennessee. Additional allegations were brought out that some companies selling building supplies to local and state governments were forced to pay for the privilege.

Sometimes called "kickbacks," other times "political payoffs" several company executives claimed that state or local officials took as much as 10% of the bidding price when awarding contracts. This could amount to tens of thousands of dollars per bid. If true, it meant that taxpayers were bilked out of millions of dollars annually.

Federal prosecutors deposed Macon County Road Supervisor Harold Cothron.

The case dragged on for more than two years in one form or another. In November, Delay family members (Wayne, Fred, and Louise), and their companies, Sherman Concrete Pipe Company, and Conway Metal Culvert Company were suing the United States government for the return of $300,000 lost to the IRS in disallowed tax deductions, fraud penalties, and interest.

The Delay family claimed they paid several Tennessee Road Supervisors for "political purposes." The Delays even produced cancelled checks to try to prove their claims that they had bribed officials. Macon County Road Supervisor Harold Cothron testified for the United States. He denied receiving any of the 11 checks the Delays produced that were made out to him and endorsed with his name. The attorney for the United States told the court that the checks were forged.

The Delays accused another Macon County official of taking money from them. Wayne Delay claimed he personally delivered one contribution to Road Commissioner Lloyd Hargis. Hargis denied receiving any contribution from Delay.

Sources:

Caldwell, Nat. "Truckers Didn't Go It Alone In Payoffs to Public Officials." *The Nashville Tennessean*, June 27, 1965.

Kenyon, Nellie. "Delay Plot Try Charged." *The Nashville Tennessean*, November 9, 1967.

Kenyon, Nellie. "Warf Aid Told in Delay Trial." *The Nashville Tennessean*, November 10, 1967.

Drowning after Prison Break.

Billy Wayne Bowman was serving a sentence of one-to-three years at the Tennessee state prison in Nashville. He had been convicted of assault with intent to commit manslaughter.

Bowman was doing "easy" time as a trustee at the minimum-security prison work farm. Bowman, who was only 22, was reported to have escaped from the prison on July 12, 1965.

Oddly enough, when relating details of Bowman's escape, Prison Warden Henry Heer didn't seem overly concerned about it. Heer stated that Bowman was the twelfth inmate to escape from the prison farm since June 1. The warden smiled as he told reporters, "I don't think it's anything unusual. Every time it gets too hot to work it happens."

Three days after his escape, at about 10 a.m. Bowman's lifeless body was found floating in the Cumberland River several miles downstream from the prison near Nashville's Commodore Yacht Club. He had evidently drowned while trying to swim the river.

Ironically, by the time Bowman's body was found, the other 11 escaped inmates had either returned to the prison on their own, or they had been recaptured.

Bowman was survived by his young wife, Margaret *Harp* Bowman, and his one-month-old son, Billy Wayne Bowman, Jr.

Sources.

"Drowning victim's rights conducted." *The Macon County Times*, July 22, 1965.

"Fugitive's Body Found in River." *The Nashville Tennessean*, July 16, 1965.

"12th Inmate Flees Prison." *The Nashville Tennessean*, July 13, 1965.

1966-1967

A Woman Shoots Her Husband.

Clifford Carver, age 42, of Red Boiling Springs was a tavern operator, but his death had nothing to do with his bar. He was shot and killed by his wife.

Macon County Sheriff, Hubert Knight, said that Louise *Brown* Carver had shot her husband at about 11 a.m. on November 28, 1965, and the man was dead on arrival at the hospital in Lafayette.

Louise said that Clifford intended to harm her and that he had chased her out of their house. She said her husband continued to pursue her on foot as she ran down Highway 52. Finally, unable to escape him, she said she turned and fired one shot from her .25-caliber automatic pistol. The round struck Clifford in the head and he fell mortally wounded. After shooting her husband, Louise walked about 300 yards to the home of Deputy Rex Gann where she gave herself up.

Sheriff Knight lodged Louise in the Macon County jail, but he said he would not charge her with anything until after Clifford's funeral. He added that he wasn't sure exactly what the charges against her would be.

Sources.

"Man Slain; Wife Held." *The Nashville Tennessean*, November 29, 1965.

"Woman Facing Murder Charge." *The Nashville Tennessean*, November 30, 1965.

A Story of Sex Tapes and Blackmail.

Everywhere, even small-town America is subject to scandals and the threat of scandals. In August 1966, Macon County was on the verge of being caught up in the web of an embarrassing scandal that threatened to destroy the reputations of several prominent Macon Countians. The story was front page news for more than two weeks and was the biggest story in Macon County in 1966, by far.

During the first days of August, the Tennessee Bureau of Identification (TBI) sent agents to the home of Norman Neil Franz Miller, age 46, and his wife Malinda, age 31, at 805 Ellington Drive in Lafayette. The agents noted that Miller, who was a school teacher and sometimes commercial photographer, lived well and had expensive tastes. Not only did Miller have a new red 1966 Austin-Healy sports car, but his house was lavishly furnished in the French provincial style.

The TBI agents applied their warrant to seize about 5,000 undeveloped photographs, a large number of audio tapes, and several pistols from the Miller home. The TBI seized the items based on a tip that Miller and his wife were using the photos and recordings for the purposes of extortion.

The dapper Franz Miller, who came to Macon County in 1962 to teach, was a smooth character. He was reputed to have connections with actors and other Hollywood movers and shakers. He had a collection of photos of himself with celebrities. He said he had once worked for Lux Radio Theater and for gossip columnist and screenwriter Louella Parsons. He also was acquainted with opera star Helen Traubel.

Miller claimed to be rather close to then recently deceased movie star Lindia Darnell. Of Darnell, Miller said, "We were just friends and she asked me to be in a picture with her."

Miller also spoke in whispers about working for a Hollywood gangster. He said he photographed society events at the mobster's mansion.

Miller appeared to be a Hollywood stereotype. He dressed in expensive suits and had a taste for the extravagant. He drove the aforementioned sports car, and, by his own admission, didn't always pay his debts.

Miller calmly denied that he was running any kind of an extortion racket.

The TBI and District Attorney General Baxter Key were mum on the matter early on, but rumors were that a Nashville physician had already been questioned and that several local people would be interviewed soon. While the investigation was ongoing, neither Miller nor his wife were charged immediately.

Enon consolidated school in rural northeastern Macon County had an enrollment of about 80. Miller had been the principal there until December 1965 when the Macon County Board of Education bought out his contract and let him go. Miller said the reason for the buyout was that parents complained about his method of discipline. "I was too strict," said Miller.

After being let go by the Macon County school system, Miller moved to Yorktown, Texas in early 1966, and taught six-graders there. Getting another teaching job was easy for him. Firstly, he was certified to teach school in Tennessee, Texas, Georgia, and Kentucky. Secondly, he had received a recommendation from the Macon County Superintendent of Schools, Doyle Gaines.

Miller tenure at Yorktown was short. He was there for only 69 days. The Yorktown principal said Miller was "weak" in matters of discipline. The principal said Miller, "told me that he liked to teach high school subjects and that he was trained for high school work. This was his reason for leaving."

Although Miller was legally qualified to teach, one would think his checkered past would have prevented him from being hired. He had been variously charged with indecent exposure, forgery and passing bad checks, breaking and entering, and grand larceny. He had been arrested in Dallas, Texas; Fort Worth, Texas; Denver, Colorado; Los Angeles, California; and Cheyene, Wyoming. Macon County Superintendent of Schools, Doyle Gaines said when the Board of Education bought out Miller's contract, they knew nothing about the principal's arrests.

Carlos Hargis, who was Superintendent of Schools in 1962, hired Miller. He said he checked Miller's references and they were good. Hargis also said he checked Miller's academic record at the University of Texas and it was good. Hargis didn't go further into Miller's background than that. Being in dire need of teachers and seeing no problem with Miller, Hargis signed him on.

Gaines readily confirmed that the school board "bought out" Miller's contract in December 1965, paying him $2,944. Gaines also admitted that buying out a teacher's contract was "not really ordinary." But he added quickly that doing so in this case may have prevented violence at Enon Elementary. Gaines said, "A lot of parents in that community were upset over the way the school was being run. There were some complaints about the way he was handling discipline."

The superintendent stated that the year before, a teacher was "beaten up something awful – they thought for a while that he was going to be crippled." Gaines continued that "things were stacking up to where" it was conceivable that Miller might face the same kind of violence.

Gaines then related that the "way the public-school law is written, it is hard to let a teacher who has tenure go. The school board voted to buy the contract, and he (Miller) agreed."

Kenneth Witcher was a member of both the Macon County Board of Education and the Tennessee legislature. Witcher and Gaines both said they'd heard rumors that before he was let go Miller had taken to carrying a pistol to school with him every day. Witcher said Miller "just wasn't able to handle the school. I don't know whether it was discipline or what it was. Lack of common sense maybe." Witcher conceded that buying out Miller's contract "was an unusual situation."

Witcher and Gaines agreed that the buyout had nothing to do with Miller's alleged extortion scheme. Gaines told reporters, "I've heard rumors, But I'm telling you what transpired. That (the extortion scheme) had nothing to do with" the buyout.

Gaines said the buyout money came from the school fund and Miller received it on December 22, 1965. Gaines justified getting rid of Miller because the teacher "admitted that he was a failure at the school."

Bank records indicated that on December 22, Miller deposited $400 in cash and a check for $2,951.65 into his local bank account. Then on December 23, Miller purchased a cashier's check in the amount of $3,000.

Gaines also admitted that two auditors from the state comptroller's office cane to Lafayette to look at the school board's financial records. Gaines said the audit was routine and it had nothing to do with the Miller transaction.

Whether the audit was connected to the Miller case in the beginning or not, it became connected to the case quickly. The auditors wanted to know what had happened to several pieces of expensive photographic equipment that were unaccounted for. Gaines said he didn't know exactly how much equipment was missing or exactly when it disappeared. He said the equipment was purchased for a class that Miller started and taught, but the class had since been cancelled.

Carlos Hargis said Miller started the class in 1962 and Gaines said it was cancelled in 1964. As Gaines remembered it, at first "the course was popular with a lot of kids. Some of them may have learned a hobby or even a vocation through it. But after a while, interest died down and it was discontinued."

Since the program had been defunct for two years, the equipment had been missing for at least that long. Gaines said that no regular inventory was ever made of any school equipment. At least one camera, an enlarger, expensive filters, stainless steel development tanks, film and chemicals were unaccounted for. On the bright side, Gaines said that the day after the teacher's house was raided, Miller returned an expensive movie projector and a tape recorder belonging to the school system.

Miller had stated that at the time of his buyout he had signed a contract in which he agreed to leave Lafayette. Superintendent Gaines said he knew of "no contract Miller signed in which he agreed to leave town." Gaines said Miller "did mention to me several times that he had no friends here and that he was going to leave."

The members of the Macon County Board of Education backed Gaines up. They denied that Miller was asked to sign any document agreeing to leave Lafayette in exchange for his buy out. Board members also agreed that the buyout was necessary because Miller had tenure.

Miller couldn't produce a copy of the document he said he was forced to sign, but he did offer a reason as to why he did it. He said he was ashamed of his police record and "certain persons threatened bring it out if I didn't agree to leave town."

The Board members said they weren't aware of Miller's brushes with the law when they bought him out. The Board produced its resolution December 14, 1965, to buy Miller's contract:

Motion by (Oren) Brooks, seconded by (Kenneth) Witcher, to supplement Franz Miller, Principal at Enon School, in the amount of $2,944 from local funds, due to the extra activities and demands upon the principal, and also due to the reputation of the school making it almost impossible to secure a certified person for this position. This action taken only because consolidation is not considered feasible because of our interest in holding the school.

It is interesting that a "supplement" was normally paid as a bonus for providing extra services, such as coaching a sports team or directing a band.

A week after passing the resolution, the School Board accepted Miller's resignation and appointed Dean Rusk principal at Enon Elementary.

A group of parents with children at Enon Elementary took offense with the contention that *they* held any responsibly for Miller's buyout. They said Miller was a "satisfactory" principal at their school and that he had no serious problems in the area of discipline. They contradicted school officials that said Miller's contract was bought out because of parental complaints. They also said they knew nothing about Miller's arrests until long after he left the school.

Speaking for the Enon parents, Robert D. Hagan said, "The kids thought as much of him (Miller) as the last principal we had. He did a lot better job than some principals we had before. We hadn't complained and there hadn't been any complaints to speak of. The first thing we knew he was released over the Christmas vacation. We didn't know they had paid him off until we read it in the paper Tuesday (August 9). We feel they are trying to push the blame off on our community. They didn't fire him for anything he did at Enon."

The parents also resented the implication that they resorted to violence in dealing with unpopular teachers. The Enon parents conceded that a teacher had been beaten there in 1964 after he spanked a child. However, they said an "outsider" had assaulted the teacher and the violent man was a member of the military who had been stationed overseas since 1965.

Despite the protestations of the Enon parents, Superintendent Gaines repeated that there had been "numerous complaints" from parents about Miller.

For his part, Miller's Enon experience seemed to have left him bitter. He said Enon had "always been a tough community, and now they're trying to look normal. I had nothing but trouble out there."

Miller had more problems than just with the TBI. He was also under investigation by the IRS. Miller admitted that over the course of the past six or seven years he had failed to report some

$30,000 to $35,000 in income from his commercial photography business. He didn't provide details, but he said there was nothing dishonest about his business.

Miller claimed that after he returned to Lafayette in 1966, a man had been pressuring him to "get out" of Lafayette. However, Miller refused to identify the man or detail the type of pressure that was being exerted. The said that if he revealed the name of the man pressuring him, another man, a friend, would be ruined. Miller attempt to prove the validity of his assertion by playing a recording of a telephone conversation with another man. The man said that if Miller didn't get out of town, he'd be shot.

The mysterious Mr. Miller was capable of and willing to make threats too. He told reporters that he had "enough information about certain individuals to put them behind bars." He stated the information was "just as close as my safety deposit box." Miller refused to show reporters what was in his safety deposit box – even if he had one. Miller went back and forth with his threats. One time he'd say his previous remarks were "untrue and a mistake." Then, he would repeat his threats again later.

Miller was not embarrassed by the fact that he had suffered from mental illness. However, he said his condition had improved since he married Malinda. He said he had been institutionalized twice in Colorado and that he had attempted suicide twice. He said that he had tried to "gas" himself once, and the other time he slashed his left arm just below the elbow with a razor blade. The second attempt came while he was in a mental hospital in Pueblo, Colorado.

The strange case of Franz Miller took another mysterious twist on August 11, 1966. It was revealed that Miller had received a large number of money orders. The money orders were purchased in 1965 and ranged in size from $10 to $100, many of them bearing fictitious names and non-existent Nashville addresses. All the money orders were drawn on Consumers

Money Order Company which allowed a maximum amount of $100. The money orders carried names such as Joe Johnson, Tom Smith, Joe Smith, and Jim Jones.

Some of the money orders were bought on the same day for the same amount. They also carried the same phony names.

Then a letter was discovered in which Miller demanded more than $100 monthly from someone. The total amount Miller allegedly wanted was $3,000. The letter was dated in 1964, and the belief was that some of money orders sent to Miller in 1965 were connected to the letter.

Miller admitted receiving the money orders, but he denied that extortion or any other illegalities were connected to them. He said he was receiving the money orders as part of an out-of-court settlement to prevent a lawsuit. He would not comment on the nature of the supposed lawsuit, but he asked. "How could anyone say it was illegal when the agreement was made as a legal contract?" He could not produce a copy of the contract.

Unable to prove what he said, Miller gave another reason for why he received the money orders, "Let's say they're from admirers who wanted to help me out financially."

Still, another strange item came to light. On October 28, 1963, Miller had made a most unusual request to the Macon County school board. Instead of taking his checks at the end of each pay period, he asked that his entire monthly salary of $385 be sent to a woman in Hickman, Kentucky. Miller told school officials that the woman worked for the Hickman County school system and he was paying off a $3,000 debt, plus 3% interest.

While the request was unique, the checks were sent to Kentucky.

During the investigation, when asked about the reason he had his pay sent to Hickman, Miller offered a different reason. "I guess it does look a little odd, doesn't it?" Said Miller. He denied he had ever owed the woman any money. Then he explained that he did it to avoid garnishment from his Macon County creditors.

The next natural question was how he lived if all his pay went to Kentucky. Miller shrugged and said, "Well, that's what looks funny."

District Attorney Baxter Key believed he had enough evidence to indict the Millers. On August 16, Key petitioned Circuit Court Judge John A. Mitchell of Cookeville to convene a special session of the grand jury at Lafayette. Mitchell granted Key's motion and called for the grand jury to convene at 9 a.m. on August 22. Rumors were swarming like biblical locust. The latest were that the investigation was spreading beyond allegations of extortion.

The Miller case was weirder than the strangest Hollywood farce and it was growing weirder by the day. After District Attorney Key obtained the order to empanel the grand jury, Franz Miller came unhinged.

At first, Miller didn't seem worried at all. He expressed his wiliness to testify before the grand jury. He told reporters that he didn't have an attorney. "I can't see that I need an attorney," he said. "I haven't done anything wrong."

Later that morning, Miller told a reporter, "I'd like to get into an airplane, push the stick, and let it spin in. But I couldn't do anything like that."

After driving to Hendersonville for unknown reasons that afternoon, Miller stopped and called his wife from a phone booth in front of Woody's Restaurant on Gallatin Road. He told her, "If I don't get back, I love you. Take care of Collette." Collette was the Miller's three-year-old daughter.

A little later, the phone rang at the front desk of the *Nashville Tennessean*. Eugene Dietz took the call and the voice on the other end said, "This is Franz Miller. Jack Corn has been trying to get in touch with me."

Jack Corn was a photographer covering the Miller case for the Tennessean. Since they shared an interest in photography, the two had several friendly conversations.

Dietz told Miller that Corn was out of the office and that when he could be contacted, he'd call Miller back.

An upset Miller responded, "He can't reach me by phone. The next time Jack Corn photographs me, I'll be dead."

Dietz contacted Corn by radio and Corn returned to the office. Worried, Corn called the Miller home in Lafayette. Malinda answered the phone. Corn asked to speak to Miller and Malinda said her husband wasn't home. Corn said the Miller seemed terribly upset when he called the *Tennessean*. Malinda burst into tears and told Corn that she didn't know where her husband was.

Corn remained in the office hoping that Miller would call again. A few minutes later, Miller did.

Miller was weeping and speaking incoherently. Miller finally told Corn, "I understand you are trying to get in touch with me. What can you possibly tell me? This is the end of it all. Nobody came help me."

Miller returned home later that evening, but he left again without telling Malinda where he was going.

His activities since Miller left his home on the evening of August 16 were certainly those of a man out of touch with reality. Miller, for reasons that never became clear, drove to Lebanon, Tennessee.

On the morning pf August 17 at about 6:30 a.m. Dr. Jack Clark saw Miller at a Lafayette eatery. Clark came up to Miller and started a conversation. The distraught school teacher who hadn't had any sleep, cried and babbled incoherently for about 15 minutes before finally saying, "They've finally stared me down."

Miller rose, went outside, got into his car, and drove toward Hartsville. Fearing that Miller intended suicide, Dr. Clark got into his own car and followed the unstable man.

Miller was driving erratically. He drove along the curvy road at speeds up to 75 miles pers hour and he drove on the wrong side of the road much of the time. After a few miles, Clark pulled over and called the Tennessee Highway Patrol. He alerted a trooper of what was happening, then Clark resumed his pursuit of Miller.

Clark came upon Miller's car parked outside a church cemetery about four miles from Lafayette. Clark located Miller wandering aimlessly. Clark convinced the exhausted school teacher to return with him to the hospital at Lafayette. Clark had Miller admitted and placed him under sedation.

Clark said Miller told him that he'd like to kill himself, but he couldn't because of his daughter. "In my opinion he (Miller) definitely needs psychiatric help," the doctor said.

District Attorney Key requested a court order to commit Miller to Central State psychiatric hospital in Nashville to evaluate "whether he is sane."

The evaluation of Miller's mental state was expected to take several days, or even weeks.

At 7:30 a.m. on August 18, Miller was charged with indecent exposure on a warrant issued by a Lebanon judge at 10:30 p.m. on August 17. Miller couldn't be served immediately because he was still under heavy sedation. He was also under guard because it was feared that he might attempt suicide.

The charge came from an incident that occurred on the evening of August 16 outside a Lebanon bowling alley between 8:30 and 8:45. He was accused of exposing himself to two girls, both of whom were 14, but the details were sketchy. The TBI agent that brought the warrant said that "because two young girls were involved" he wouldn't bring them any undue embarrassment by providing very many details to the press.

What could be learned was that the two girls said they were approached by a man outside the bowling alley and that he exposed himself to them. The TBI "had some information called in" to it by a truck driver who witnessed the incident, and upon investigation, the two girls identified a photograph of Miller.

The TBI agent said he couldn't account for Miller's activities between 8:45 p.m. on August 16 and 6:30 a.m. on August 17 when Dr. Clark saw Miller at the restaurant.

While Miller's commitment to the mental institution might affect the indecent exposure charge against him, District Attorney Key said the grand jury investigation of the teacher and his wife would go on as scheduled.

The dark-eyed, dark-haired beauty, Malinda Miller departed her home on August 18 after her husband was committed to mental institution. She apparently took her daughter with her. No one was certain where she went.

Malinda likely felt she had to leave. Franz Miller had told a reporter on August 17 that the lease on his house would expire in four days, "I'm going to have to move," he said. "I don't have any money." He also said he had previously declared bankruptcy.

The first reports were that Malinda was going to Nashville to rent an apartment and find a job. However, that's not what happened. An anonymous caller to the *Tennessean* told a reporter, "She's not in Nashville." Some of her furniture was sent to a Nashville storage unit, however.

Malinda was last seen driving her husband's sports car. It had personal belongings strapped to it.

Since the story first broke, reporters had learned a great deal about the woman called Malinda Miller. In 1961, she apparently abandoned her husband and two young daughters, ages 8 and 3, in Hickman, Kentucky. She then ran away with Franz Miller.

Malinda, whose name was actually Betty June Morrow, had been deeply involved with the Hickman First Church of God. She seemed to be the dutiful housewife. Her first husband said that during their marriage of nine years, "She always had a good meal on the table when I got home. She kept the house clean and neat and she was a good mother."

On the other hand, Malinda kept her husband drained of cash. She loved nice clothes and fancy furniture. She constantly spent more than her husband could afford. She was also fascinated by all things French and she and her first husband quarreled when she wanted to give their children French names.

Betty June dropped her children off at her sister's house on April 18, 1961, and never saw or talked to them again. Instead of going back for her children, she moved into a hotel room with Franz Miller.

About a month before Malinda moved in with Franz, he had photographed the cast of a play she was in. She seemed enthralled by the fact that Miller knew movie stars. According to her first husband, "Betty changed after that, but I never suspected a thing. Some days she wouldn't even be home when I came home for supper, but I never asked her about where she had been."

Her first husband divorced Malinda on May 2, 1961, and he was granted custody of their children. Malinda never asked for permission to visit the children.

The TBI released word that they were trying to learn the identity of a man photographed lying on a sofa with a woman. Agents believed the man could provide new leads in the Miller case. The photographed man turned out to be Franz Miller.

While there were many loose ends in the case, on August 19, District Attorney Key said he would ask the grand jury to indict Franz and Malinda Miller on charges of extortion, grand larceny, and a "crime against nature." Key said that other charges might be brought against the Millers as well. The grand larceny charge stemmed from the photographic equipment the school system auditors couldn't locate. Under Tennessee law, a "crime against nature" was any sexual act that wasn't "normal."

The District Attorney said he would call 15 people to testify before the grand jury. Some of his witnesses would be members of the Macon County School Board, so said Key.

The grand jury at Lafayette met for six hours and then, as expected, indicted Franz and Malinda. But there was some drama before that happened. When insurance agency owner, Howard A. Smith, was called to testify he balked at doing so. After a meeting between District Attorney Key, Smith, and Smith's attorney, the insurance man agreed to testify. He answered questions for about fifteen minutes.

A local furniture dealer provided a package containing an audio tape to TBI Agent R. C. Goodwin. Both the furniture dealer and Goodwin testified before the grand jury. In all, Key only called seven witnesses. None of the school board members took the stand.

The Millers were jointly indicted on three counts of extortion and one count of a crime against nature. Kenneth Witcher of Red Boiling Springs, Howard A. Smith of Lafayette, and Dr. Fred Overton of Nashville were identified in the indictments as victims of separate extortion schemes.

The Millers allegedly used tape recordings to attempt to extort $1,200 from Witcher by threatening to accuse him of having illicit sexual relations with Malinda.

Another indictment charged that the Millers ran the same scheme to try to extort $1,000 from Smith.

The Millers allegedly received some $1,865 of the $3,000 they demanded from Overton. According to the grand jury, the Millers threatened to accuse Overton of performing an illegal abortion on Malinda if he didn't pay them. The evidence in the Overton case included a letter from Franz Miller to Overton dated December 13, 1964.

The crime against nature charge was apparently based on a photo Franz took of himself with Malinda.

District Attorney Key said that the investigation was ongoing, but Franz Miller's alleged "secret list" of 30 people involved in his schemes wasn't part of it. Miller claimed that he had a "list" of 30 people involved in crimes and he had threatened to expose them and "drag a lot of people down." The TBI and the District Attorney doubted that such a list existed. District Attorney Key said, "There are some more people who will be questioned, but talk of a secret list of 30 people is silly."

Miller offered his list to *Macon County Times* editor, Charlie Gregory. Gregory turned him down. He said that even if the list existed, nothing could be verified. Gregory had too much integrity to damage people's reputations based on Miller's unsubstantiated claims.

Reporters from the *Tennessean* asked Miller for the list, but he never produced it.

When the Millers were indicted on August 22, Franz was still in the mental institution and Malinda was still missing. Malinda's sister was in Nashville looking for clues as to where the pretty fugitive might be. Malinda's sister said, "Something happened to her in that hotel. Almost overnight she seemed to become a completely different person."

Malinda didn't remain free for long. On the evening of August 23, acting on an anonymous tip, the TBI arrested her in Memphis. She was taken to Jackson, Tennessee and then transported back to Lafayette.

Of course, even Malinda's stay in jail took on a surreal aspect. She was unable to make her $2,000 bond and was put in a cell at the Macon County jail. After being in the jail at Lafayette for only a few hours, Malinda complained about her lodgings and requested "better quarters." Macon County Sheriff Hubert Knight obliged her. He transported her to the Smith County jail at Carthage which offered "modern facilities."

Malinda's stay in the Carthage jail wasn't long either. Four Clay County "strangers" put up her $2,000 bond on August 25. James Reneau III, Malinda's attorney, said some of her friends had called and asked for his help in getting her freed. He then called four friends of his. "They signed it (the bond) at my request," he said. "They don't even know the woman."

Reneau told reporters that Malinda planned to enter a plea of not guilty. "We are convinced of Mrs. Miller's innocence," he said. Reneau was not representing Franz Miller. Reneau continued that he'd move for Malinda to have a trial separate from Franz's. District Attorney Key said he'd oppose the severance motion.

The Millers were scheduled to go on trial on November 21, but it was in doubt. If Franz Miller had not been declared competent to stand trial, proceedings would have to be postponed until at least March 1967.

The doctors at Central State delayed making any decision about Franz Miller for as long as they could. Finally, on November 19, the doctors relayed to the court that Miller's mental condition was such that he could stand trial. "But we feel it would set him back if he goes on trial at this time. All the publicity in this case has had an adverse effect on him and we feel that the publicity of a trial at this time would be detrimental to his condition." However, the doctors continued that "it shouldn't be too long before he is ready to be released."

The District Attorney didn't argue the point, and the trial was rescheduled for March 1967. But Reneau engaged in some legal maneuvering during the rescheduling hearing on November 22.

Reneau motioned to have the charges against his client, Malinda Miller, dismissed. Judge John A. Mitchell rejected the motion out of hand.

Then Reneau moved to have the evidence seized during the raid on the Miller home suppressed. Reneau said two factors rendered the search warrant invalid. First, the warrant stated that a search was to be conducted at 900 Ellington Drive, but the residence searched was several doors down at 805. Second, according to Reneau, the warrant failed to carry the name of the informant whose tip caused it to be filed. Reneau requested an immediate ruling on his motion.

Judge Mitchell refused to rule on the motion to suppress at that time. He told the opposing attorneys, "I decline to hear it at this time. I think it would be unwise because of the absence of the defendants."

Reneau countered that "We have no assurance that the other defendant (Franz Miller) will ever be in this courtroom."

The judge still refused to rule on the motion, but the persistent defense attorney would not take no for an answer. He summoned five witnesses to testify in support of his motion, but the judge wouldn't let them take the stand. He said, "it would be a waste of time."

Mitchell did promise Reneau that he would rule on the motion to suppress before the case went to trial in March. However, he never ruled on the motion.

District Attorney Baxter Key scoffed at Reneau's histrionics. Key said he wasn't worried that the judge would rule for the defense on the suppression motion. Key said, "We might not even use the evidence taken in the raid." Then Key confided, "We can present the evidence we have in less than three hours."

The Miller case grew weirder still in February 1967. A new issue flared up when Tennessee State Attorney General, George McCanless, had his office notify the Macon County school board that that it had acted without authority when it purchased the contract of an employee (Franz Miller). The notification also stated that $2,559.60 of the $2,944 paid to Miller had to be returned to the general school fund.

The school board was let off the hook for the money. Never identified "friends" repaid the buyout of Franz Miller's contract to the school system.

When asked who paid repaid the buyout, the Macon County school board chairman, Lewis Gross answered, "I don't know." Gross opined that the private citizens probably repaid the buyout because they agreed with the board's original decision. "I don't know who it was," he said, "but it must have been quite a few of them. I think the people who did it thought the board did right buying the contract."

When asked if the school board would try to get the money back from Miller, Gross answered, "I don't imagine he has it." Gross also said that school board members wouldn't repay the "friends" because "we wouldn't know who to pay it back to." Gross added that he was unaware that the board's obligation had been relieved until he was informed of the reimbursement by the attorney general's office.

School board member and one of the targets of the extortion plot, Kenneth Witcher refused to comment on the repayment.

The money was repaid through the Macon County Trustee's office. Officials refused to say who made the payment except to state that they were private citizens other than school board members.

Macon County Trustee Warren "Dub" Tucker when asked who repaid the buyout responded, "I couldn't say, but the receipt for the money was made out to 'Friends.'" Tucker added, I can't say who they were, but I think if they thought it was necessary, they would have come through with $20,000 dollars.

State Attorney General George McCanless said, "I don't think it matters (about who repaid the buyout) as long as the public funds were restored." McCanless said he didn't intend to look any deeper into the matter. His only concern had been the return of the public funds. McCanless conceded that it was unusual for private citizens to assume the board's obligations. Then he added quickly, "I suppose the whole case is unusual, but I don't see anything wrong with it."

Regardless who kicked in the money, the school board was reimbursed for the money it paid to buy out Miller and the taxpayers weren't out anything.

The preliminary hearing in the Miller case was to begin on March 20, 1967. Malinda's attorney, James Reneau III intended to call three Macon County officials and two charity drive chairs. Their testimony would, so hoped Reneau, prove that a change of venue was needed to obtain a fair trial for his client.

Reneau said he became convinced that a change of venue was necessary when he learned that private citizens had reimbursed the Macon County school board the amount of the buyout it had paid Miller. Reneau was certain that the payment by "friends" prejudiced the case against Malinda.

Reneau said, "If they can raise this kind of money in a few hours, when they only got about $1,700 during the Heart Fund drive with 100 volunteers working several weeks, I think it shows an unusual interest in the case. Frankly, I'm scared we can't get a fair trial, especially after somebody said they could have raised $20,000 if necessary."

Reneau said he'd initiated subpoenas for County Judge J. G. (James Goldman) Austin, Macon County Trustee Warren "Dub" Tucker, and Lewis Gross, the chairs of the local Heart Fund and Cerebral Palsy drives, and others. County Court Clerk Hillas Swindle confirmed that he had prepared subpoenas for a dozen individuals.

Franz Miller's attorney, Public Defender James A. Donoho of Hartsville, concurred with the motion to change venue.

The trial hit a snag on the evening of March 19, when Malinda was reported to be seriously ill. She was admitted to the Clay County Hospital at Celina. Malinda's attorney said he learned of her illness for the first time from her doctor who called and said she was in the hospital. Reneau told reporters, "I understand it's pretty serious. I'm going to see her and see her doctor before deciding about Monday's trial."

Malinda's doctor, with her permission, stated that she was suffering from a pelvic infection and infection of the female organs. The doctor said the infection could have come "from the bloodstream, local spreading from other parts of the body, or intercourse. We are unable to tell."

Malinda was expected to be well enough to leave the hospital in a week or so.

Later, Reneau said he didn't intend to ask for a postponement. "I would like to go ahead and get the preliminary hearing out of the way, especially this issue about a change of venue," he said. "I have no plans to call Mrs. Miller for this anyway."

Malinda had arrived in Celina on March 17. She had been living with her mother in Trenton, Kentucky and working at a shoe factory there. After arriving in Celina, Malinda stayed at Reneau's "fishing camp" until she became ill.

On March 20, Judge Mitchell heard arguments for a change of venue. The defense produced several witnesses who endeavored to show that the Miller affair had received "more publicity than any other case in the history of Macon County." One witness, Wallace J. Prenzell of Nashville testified that he had "made studies" of the effect of publicity on the outcome of criminal cases, introduced more than twenty editions of Nashville newspapers carrying stories on the case into evidence.

Defense attorney James Donoho then took the stand. He testified that the locals were "afraid" of the Miller case. Donoho told the court, "I questioned a prominent citizen and asked him if he thought Miller could get a fair trial. He took off running like someone was after him. There is some kind of undercurrent in this case in which you can't get people to talk about it." Donoho finished, "You know why no one would express an opinion? They were afraid someone would say they are on Miller's side. That is the fear in Macon County."

The defense had intended to call Warren "Dub" Tucker, Lewis Gross, and Doyle Gaines to testify. However, Macon County Sheriff, Maburn Dyer said he'd been unable to serve any of them with subpoenas. Dyer said he'd been looking for the trio for three days, and he'd just learned that they had "gone to Nashville about getting a college to come here."

James Donoho wasn't buying it. Speaking sharply, Donoho told the court, "I would say it's very unusual for a trustee, a school board chairman, and a school director to be out of town on Saturday, Sunday, and Monday – very unusual and more than a coincidence."

The District Attorney wasn't particularly opposed to the change of venue, but he did point out that "Most of the (newspaper) articles deal with quotations from the defendants themselves. When they (reporters) are told these things by the defendants, they have a right to print it. This is a case where the defendant has made his own bed – let him lie in it."

Judge Mitchell listened to the arguments and then surprised no one when he ordered the trial moved to Lebanon.

District Attorney General Key said he would try the Mitchells on the crime against nature charge on April 17, "see how it comes out, and then try the extortion cases."

The crime against nature case was problematic. The court would have to decide whether a consenting husband and wife could engage with each other in a crime against nature.

Key said he would have the tape recordings seized during the raid on the Miller home in August 1966 transcribed so the defense could read them.

Also on March 20, a newly empaneled grand jury in Lafayette indicted the Millers on a fourth count of extortion. The "True Bill" stated that the Millers extorted $1,000 from Carthage paving contractor Ernest Haggard Price. The charge said that the Millers threatened to accuse Price, who later gave up his business and moved to Nashville, of having sex with Malinda if he didn't pay the money.

The indictment read: "About August 1, 1962 the Millers willfully, feloniously, and maliciously threatened to accuse Ernest Haggard Price of an immoral act, to wit: an illicit affair with Betty June Morrow Miller, alias Malina Miller with intent to extort and did extort $1,000" from him.

The trial didn't get underway on April 17. The court convened on April 24. Onlookers in the Lebanon courtroom expected juicy details that not even a television soap opera could rival. However, they were denied their entertainment. The case that had kept so many enthralled for eight months was over in a flash.

The District Attorney and defense lawyers met for four hours hammering out a deal. Malinda's attorneys James Reneau Jr. and James Reneau III contended that she was innocent because Franz Miller had recorded her and the extortion victims without her knowledge. Key agreed to drop the charges against Malinda, provided Franz entered a guilty plea.

After the prosecution agreed to drop charges against Malinda, Franz Miller entered a guilty plea to three counts of extortion. He accepted a rather light sentence of two to five years.

District Attorney Key said he was pleased with the plea and he dropped the crime against nature, indecent exposure, and one extortion charge.

Miller said he admitted his guilt for his daughter. "That is what it was all for – Collette to be with her mother, A child needs her mother."

On her way out of the courtroom, Malinda told reporters, "I'm relieved it's all over." She said she intended to return to Clinton, Kentucky, and go back to work in the shoe factory where several of her relatives were employed.

Franz Miller wanted out of prison as quickly as possible. He had stayed out of trouble and had earned his first parole hearing on November 28, 1967. District Attorney Key said he wouldn't oppose Miller' parole. Miller said that if he was paroled, he intended to move to Memphis and work as a commercial photographer there. He also related that his arrest and conviction had wrecked his marriage. He appeared surprised that Malinda had not visited him in prison.

The parole board postponed a decision on releasing Miller pending an examination by the prison psychiatrist. However, the examination was a nothing more than a formality and Miller was quickly released.

Sources:

Blankenship, Harold G. *History of Macon County, Tennessee.* Tompkinsville, Kentucky: Monroe County Press, 1986.

"Board Sets Hearing for Extortionist." *The Nashville Tennessean*, November 22, 1967.

Daughtrey, Larry and Frank Gibson. "4 Indictments In Macon." *The Nashville Tennessean*, August 23, 1966.

Daughtrey, Larry and Frank Gibson. "Jury To Probe Miller Case." *The Nashville Tennessean*, August 16, 1966.

Daughtrey, Larry and Frank Gibson. "Macon Board Hunts School Photo Gear." *The Nashville Tennessean*, August 13, 1966.

Daughtrey, Larry and Frank Gibson. "Malinda in Smith County Jail." *The Nashville Tennessean*, August 25, 1966.

Daughtrey, Larry and Frank Gibson. "Malinda Plans Not Guilty Plea." *The Nashville Tennessean*, September 1, 1966.

Daughtrey, Larry and Frank Gibson. "Malinda Seized in Memphis." *The Nashville Tennessean*, August 24, 1966.

Daughtrey, Larry and Frank Gibson. "Miller Charged In Wilson Warrant." *The Nashville Tennessean*, August 18, 1966.

Daughtrey, Larry and Frank Gibson. "Miller 'Secret' List Denied." *The Nashville Tennessean*, September 2, 1966.

Daughtrey, Larry and Frank Gibson. "Miller's Contract Bought for $2,944." *The Nashville Tennessean*, August 12, 1966.

Daughtrey, Larry and Frank Gibson. "Miller's Letter Trade Probe." *The Nashville Tennessean*, August 15, 1966.

Daughtrey, Larry and Frank Gibson. "Money Orders Flood to Miller." *The Nashville Tennessean*, August 12, 1966.

Daughtrey, Larry and Frank Gibson. "'This is the End,' Miller Crys." *The Nashville Tennessean*, August 17, 1966.

Daughtrey, Larry. "'Miller Not Paid To Leave'" *The Nashville Tennessean*, August 10, 1966.

Daughtrey, Larry and Frank Gibson. "Miller's Contract Bought for $2,944." *The Nashville Tennessean*, August 12, 1966.

Daughtrey, Larry and Frank Gibson. "Parents, Pupils 'Liked' Miller." *The Nashville Tennessean*, August 9, 1966.

Daughtrey, Larry. "Miller Case Probe Grows." *The Nashville Tennessean*, August 20, 1966.

Daughtrey, Larry. "Mysterious Professor Miller Makes Macon Hum." *The Nashville Tennessean*, August 12, 1966.

Dawson, Ralph. "Who Bought Miller Pact." *The Nashville Tennessean*, March 18, 1967.

"Extortionist Parole Decision Postponed." *The Nashville Tennessean*, November 29, 1967.

Gibson, Frank, and Larry Daughtrey. "Young Sister Joins Search for Malinda." *The Nashville Tennessean*, August 22, 1966.

Gibson, Frank. "Extortion Trial Set For Millers." *The Nashville Tennessean*, October 22, 1966.

Gibson, Frank. "First Husband Recalls Malunda." *The Nashville Tennessean*, August 21, 1966.

Gibson, Frank. "Judge Delays Miller Trial Until March." *The Nashville Tennessean*, November 23, 1966.

Gibson, Frank. "Malinda Released On Strangers' Bond" *The Nashville Tennessean*, August 26, 1966.

Gibson, Frank. "Photos, Tapes Held in raid on Teacher." *The Nashville Tennessean*, August 8, 1966.

"Lawyers Seek Miller Trial Venue Change." *The Nashville Tennessean*, March 19, 1967.

"Malinda Miller Hospitalized in Clay County." *The Nashville Tennessean*, March 20, 1967.

"Miller Health to Delay Trial." *The Nashville Tennessean*, November 20, 1966.

Sutherland, Frank. "Malinda Freed; Franz Given 2 to 5 Years." *The Nashville Tennessean*, April 25, 1967.

Sutherland, Frank. "Venue Change Shifts Miller Trial to Wilson." *The Nashville Tennessean*, March 21, 1967.

A Scam?

A strange advertisement for a salesman appeared in Nashville newspapers. Applicants were expected to be "presentable and married." Those wishing a position were told to bring their wives to Lafayette's Ellington Hotel (now called the Budget Inn) and speak with a man identified as "Mister Roberts." Interviews were to take place on October 8 and 9, 1966, between 5:30 and 8:30 p.m.

Source:

"Salesmen." *The Nashville Tennessean*, October 11, 1966.

Youth Protesters.

On the evenings of July 23 and 24, 1966, there were youthful protesters marching in Lafayette. One might imagine that the demonstrators were protesting the war in Vietnam, or racial inequalities, but they weren't. They were upset because they believed a friend of theirs had been wrongly arrested by the police. Some thought the arrested man was "roughed up" by the arresting officers.

On Saturday night, July 23, the Lafayette police arrested Larry East, age 21. East's perceived treatment angered some and soon some 150 people, mostly teenagers led by a cadre of older men decided to "march on city hall" and to riot unless they got their way. The Lafayette Police thought the situation was made more volatile because, according them, demonstration leaders were "drinking heavily." Macon Sheriff deputies and members of the Tennessee Highway Patrol came to the aide of the Lafayette police. No riot occurred, but tensions remained high.

On July 24, about 50 youths were "milling around" on the Lafayette Public Square when a second clash happened. Unbiased observers said that a rookie member of the Lafayette Police Department approached a 23-year-old man and a dispute occurred. Lafayette police, whose station was only a few yards from the incident, rushed to the scene. However, the police officers were badly outnumbered and if the clash became violent, they would be overwhelmed.

Sheriff deputies, were also stationed only a few yards from the scene of the potential melee. They left the county jail and rushed to support the police, but even more help was needed. A radio call to the Tennessee Highway Patrol brought troopers to the scene.

Luckily, the show of force, and some calm heads, prevented what could have developed into a tragic event. The tense situation ended relatively peaceably and although they were still angry, the young people went home.

Source:

"New Clashes Hit Lafayette." *The Nashville Tennessean*, July 25, 1966.

Milk Wars.

There was a war of sorts between some members of the National Farmers Organization (NFO) and nonunion farmers. The NFO declared a "milk strike" and the nonunion producers attempted to deliver their product anyway. The battle got out of hand and some NFO members ambushed milk trucks across Tennessee.

Early in the morning of March 23, 1967, Hazel E. Goodman, age 21, and Jimmy Doss, age 26, both of Lafayette, were hauling 4,000 gallons of Grade A milk to Nashville's Pure Milk Company. when they nearly became casualties of the milk war.

Goodman and Doss drove for Hazel's father, General Sessions Judge, W. E. Goodman of Lafayette. Hazel told the story of what happened. He said it started before the truck hit the road that morning. "We have had several threatening calls from men who would not identify themselves. Monday night, (March 20) one caller said, 'if you put them trucks on the road, we'll blow 'em all to hell, and the drivers, too.'

"Last night (March 22), one of those anonymous callers told my father to keep his trucks off the road a few days."

W. E. Goodman wasn't willing to be scared off the road and about 3 a.m. on March 23, Hazel and Jimmy left Lafayette with their load of milk. About 3.5 miles from Hartsville, they saw a man running down a side road toward them. The man was carrying hunting rifle. "We heard a thump," Goodman said, "but we didn't know for sure what it was until later. A car began following us with lights on bright, so Jimmy opened the door to see what kind of car it was. The car stopped, a man got out and fired. The bullet hit the steel ladder going to the top of the tank. A small fragment hit him (Doss) on the wrist."

Goodman and Doss continued on to Hartsville and reported the incident to City Police Officer, Raymond Witcher. A few minutes later, the car that had been following the milk tanker drove up. Goodman and Doss identified it immediately. Officer Witcher searched the car. He found a .30-06 inside. The two men, Nelvin Ogen Stinson of Westmoreland and Bobby Smith of Lafayette, said they had been hunting groundhogs. Witcher confiscated the rifle but released the two suspected shooters until 10 a.m. when they were supposed to go before a judge.

It wasn't the first time that W. E. Goodman had a truck ambushed. On March 20, a W. E. Goodman truck driven by Billy White was stopped by 15 men on Highway 31-E between Glasgow, Kentucky and Hiseville, Kentucky. The ambushers didn't harm White, but they dumped half of his 2,000 gallon load and poured shoe polish into the rest.

Despite the clear danger, Hazel Goodman was defiant. "As long as producers have milk, and they want us to haul it, we'll continue to run," he said.

In what first appeared to be a simple case, it dragged on for years. In 1970, a grand jury finally indicted Stinson and Smith on three criminal counts.

Count one accused Stinson and Smith of "maliciously or wantonly shooting a missile calculated to produce death or bodily harm at or into a vehicle occupied or being used by other persons."

Count two accused the defendants of attempting to prevent Goodman and Doss from selling and delivering farm products (milk) to a Nashville processing plant.

Count three charged that the defendants advised or incited others or conspired with others to prevent the delivery of milk.

The trial was scheduled to get underway on March 18, 1970, almost three years to the day after the alleged shooting. Judge Hillard Roberts was to preside. But the lawyer for Stinson and Smith was determined that there would be no trial at all. James Reneau Jr. said his clients would plead not guilty, but he said he'd file a preliminary motion to quash the indictment on the grounds that it was "vague and uncertain."

Sources.

"Macon Milk Strike Shooting Trial Gets Under Way Today." *The Nashville Tennessean*, March 18, 1967.

"Trucker Pledges Milk Hauling Will Continue." *The Nashville Tennessean*, March 23, 1967.

1968-1969

Little Boy Set Free.

On January 25, 1968, Roy Lee Sewell sat in a Nashville courtroom. The eight-year-old lad had dark eyes, he weighed about 40 pounds, and he stood maybe three feet tall. Roy Lee didn't look much like a person that should be locked away. All Roy Lee wanted this day was to go home.

This wasn't Roy Lee's first day in court. Four months earlier, a judge in Lafayette had sent him away to the reform school called the "Tennessee Preparatory School" (TPS) for an indefinite term.

At this hearing, his parents and their attorney asked Nashville Circuit Court Judge Don R. Binkley to release the boy immediately in a proceeding, called a "habeas corpus hearing." Roy Lee didn't care about all that. He just wanted to go home.

The Sewell family was represented by James Reneau III of Carthage. Reneau charged that the order committing Roy Lee to the Tennessee Preparatory School "indefinitely" was the product of a "kangaroo court." Reneau continued that the ruling by Judge J. G. Austin was a "travesty of justice." Judge Austin's order sending Roy Lee to juvenile jail stated, "this boy is out of control of his parents and is committing depredations on private property."

Roy Lee was sent to the reform school because of an incident that happened on September 9, 1967, in which a parked truck was allegedly damaged. Roy Lee and his parents denied that he was involved in the vandalism. When asked by a reporter if he damaged the truck, Roy Lee answered, "No, sir. They just accused us."

When Roy Lee said "us" he was referring to himself and Roger Stafford. Stafford was sent to TPS for damaging the truck too, but his parents, Claude and Martha Stafford, weren't trying to get him freed.

Roy Lee's father, Bethel Emmit Sewell, age 58, was a poor man. He took the stand to defend his son. Under cross-examination by Assistant State Attorney General, George W. McHenry, Bethel testified that his family's only source of income was his monthly pension check from the Navy of $119. He said that his family also received food stamps. Bethel said he hadn't sought employment since 1956. He stated that he couldn't work because he suffered from "ulcers and joint problems." "I'm weak inside – I stick together inside," he said.

The elder Sewell said that Roy Lee was accused of breaking the truck's turn signal, and stealing some tools, but that the child was innocent.

When McHenry asked if Roy Lee had ever been in trouble before, Bethel answered, "No, sir. None of the Sewells have – none of the whole generation."

Roy Lee's mother, Francis Sewell testified next. She said that Roy Lee was sent to reform school without any evidence being presented against him.

Roy Lee's parents said they were never served with a summons or advised of their right to have an attorney present at the hearing in Lafayette. They said that Judge Austin had intended to try the case in the living room of an apartment at the Macon County jail on the night of the incident. However, a blaring police radio made it impossible for anyone to hear anything being said. Judge Austin postponed the hearing until September 12 and conducted it in his office. The Sewells said that no witness testified against Roy Lee.

Speaking of the September 12 hearing, Francis Sewell testified that Austin had a "paper against Roy Lee, but they never read it to us. We weren't informed of our rights in no way at all." The "paper" Francis spoke of was a petition signed by J. D. Hudson of Red Boiling Springs on September 11. Hudson, a part owner of the truck, asked that Roy Lee be declared delinquent.

Roy Lee was put on the witness stand, but the child burst into tears and the judge moved the hearing to his chambers. Roy Lee testified there.

Back in open court, TPS Superintendent Charles Barham testified that Roy Lee's papers were in order when he arrived there. "We don't question the decision of the court," Barham said. He continued that Roy Lee was a "good little fellow" and he didn't cause any trouble.

Barham added that while Roy Lee was at TPS it was discovered that he suffered from "inner ear trouble," and that he was being treated for it. Barham told the court, "I think for the welfare of the child he needs to stay here where he can be treated."

Before presenting his case, McHenry asked for a continuation so he could prepare the state's response to Reneau's allegations. McHenry said he didn't receive the writ of habeas corpus until the previous day.

Barham affirmed that he received the writ on January 15. He said he sent it to State Education Commissioner J. Howard Warf at 8:30 a.m. the next morning. "It went straight to the Commissioner," Barham told the judge.

Sheepishly, McHenry told the judge that after the writ went to Warf, "somehow it was misplaced."

Warf said he didn't receive the writ until January 18. But he didn't state why it took him almost a week to pass it on to McHenry even after he did receive it. A spokesman for the Tennessee Department of Education said, "We don't know why. We are checking on the reasons."

Judge Binkley wouldn't delay the habeas corpus hearing until the next term of court, but he did allow a short delay. He told McHenry to be prepared with the state's answer "no later than one week from today."

The boy was returned to the reform school to wait for the grownups to work everything out.

Judge Austin wasn't at the hearing, but he did agree to answer questions from a reporter the next day. Austin denied that he had trampled upon anyone's constitutional rights. He then asserted angrily, "We are not running a kangaroo court up here. The only thing I care about is that the boy gets the right shake about it."

Austin, who doubled as juvenile court judge, contradicted much of what the Sewells said. He said that three witnesses testified against Roy Lee, but he didn't name them. Austin also contended that he did inform the Sewells that they *could* have a lawyer present. "We tell all the cases that come in here," he said.

Austin first told the reporter that Roy Lee had damaged "a U.S. Mail truck." However, he corrected himself and said the truck was a private vehicle owned by an individual with a contract to deliver mail. Austin said, "There was no valuable mail taken." The when asked if *any* mail was stolen, Austin answered, "It wasn't brought up in the trial."

When asked what damage Roy Lee did to the truck, Austin said that the truck's keys were taken, delaying the driver's scheduled trip to Nashville. Austin didn't mention anything about a broken turn signal or stolen tools.

Still perturbed, Austin said, "This is not the only incident involved" in sending Roy Lee to reform school. "The boy wouldn't be down there if it was." When asked if Roy Lee had been in trouble before, Austin snapped, "Not trouble, but delinquency." However, Austin didn't provide any details.

On January 29, there was another hearing before Judge Binkley. The hearing took less than half an hour. McHenry told the judge that the state agreed with Reneau that Roy Lee should be released. He admitted that the way Roy Lee was incarcerated was "inconsistent" with the recent Gault decision rendered by the Supreme Court.

The Gault decision was handed down by the US Supreme Court on May 15, 1967. In it, the High Court ruled that juveniles charged with crimes were entitled to the same due process rules under the Fourteenth Amendment as adults were.

McHenry said he had spoken with Judge Austin. While McHenry didn't agree that Austin was operating a "kangaroo court," he said, "We believe the authorities up there recognize their error."

When asked if the ruling would affect the Roger Stafford case, Judge Austin said he'd review it. "I certainly try to do what is right for the children."

Judge Binkley had no choice but to release Roy Lee. However, the judge expressed concern that Roy Lee might not receive the continuing treatment he needed for his ear defect. Reneau assured the judge that the Cordell Hull Economic Opportunity Corporation had agreed to provide Roy Lee's transportation to and from Nashville so he could continue treatments. That satisfied the judge and he concluded the hearing.

As the hearing concluded, Francis Sewell asked her attorney, "We get to go home with him tonight?"

"Right now," Reneau replied.

Sources:

Elder, Rob. "Macon Judge Defends Action Committing Boy as Delinquent." *The Nashville Tennessean*, January 27, 1968.

Elder, Rob. "Parents Urge Son's Release." *The Nashville Tennessean*, January 26, 1968.

Elder, Rob. "State admits Error; Boy, 8, Freed." *The Nashville Tennessean*, January 30, 1968.

Fugitive Arrested.

On July 27, 1968, the FBI announced that agents had arrested a fugitive named Charles V. Duncan, age 39. Duncan was taken into custody in Illinois,

Duncan was charged in a federal warrant issued in Nashville on February 27 for unlawful flight to avoid prosecution. Duncan was indicted in Macon County in 1967 for first degree burglary but jumped bail before his trial.

Source:

"Tennessee Man Arrested in Ill." *The Nashville Tennessean*, July 28, 1968.

Stabbed to Death.

No place on earth populated by humans is immune to violence. However, violence in big cities is naturally more prevalent than in small towns and after moving to big cities small-town folk are often victimized.

At about 5 p.m. on August 18, 1968, residents of a Nashville apartment building heard loud groans coming from the room occupied by Wesley Treveland Shrum, and they went inside to investigate. Shrum, age 36, a Macon County native, was found face down on the floor. When his neighbors rolled him over, they saw a knife protruding from his abdomen.

Shrum was on the verge of death when he was found and he died before reaching Nashville's Baptist Hospital.

Shrum was survived by his wife, Mary Ann Bly Shrum and their three sons.

Source:

"Wesley Shrum Dies Of Knife Wounds." *The Macon County Times*, August 22, 1968.

Macon Man Indicted.

On February 1, 1969, a Davidson County grand jury indicted David L. Bergdorf of Lafayette for escaping from prison. Bergdorf allegedly strolled away from a work gang in June 1968 and fled to Kentucky.

Bergdorf remained on the run for six months until December 1968 when he was finally apprehended by FBI agents in Louisville, Kentucky. Bergdorf had been serving a one-year term in the Tennessee State Pentamery for forgery. Ironically, had he remained in custody and simply done his time, By February he would have been released.

Source:

"4 Men Indicted In Urich Slaying." *The Nashville Tennessean*, February 2, 1969.

A Possible Investigation.

On May 16, officials at the Cordell Hull Equal Opportunity Corporation and the Atlanta office of the Office of Economic Opportunity (OEO) denied that an investigation of the Macon County program was underway. Members of the Atlanta office denied the alleged investigation of a transfer of funds in the Lafayette office. They said that the visit by Fred Head had merely made a "routine field trip" to Macon County and that there was no investigation.

Yet, the day before when Head arrived in Macon County, he told reporters, "The people in the program were notified by the Atlanta office that I was coming and they were given the reason for the visit. I'm here to inquire into the possible use of funds beyond the flexibility authorized by the grantor."

Rumors were swirling that Head came to Macon County "to find out what was happening" with the Cordell Hull program. The story was that Head had uncovered evidence that "funds had been shifted from one department to another and were causing a big mix-up in accounting." The allegation was that the shift of "$52,000" meant that "people were paid from one account who never worked in that division at all." The $52,000 was a big chunk of the $360,000 that the Cordell Hull program had spent up to that point in 1969.

Frieda Biles of Red Boiling Springs had been the Executive Director of the Cordell program since its inception in September 1965. She took offense at allegations. Biles said there had been "nothing out of order regarding the handling of funds by this office. There has been no misappropriations. There has been no investigation and no audit by Mr. Head. The nature of what he said to me concerned overall program operations. There has been no shift in funds."

Without naming names, Biles claimed that there were "a couple of individuals" behind the rumors and that "someone is looking for something to pick at."

On May 25, 13 of the 45 directors of the Cordell Hull program requested that the Atlanta office of the OEO audit the Cordell Hull program. The letter addressed to OEO District Supervisor Roy Jones requested that "This audit be complete and detailed." It also requested that "a copy be made available for our inspection."

The letter was signed by the following: Carthage Mayor James Clay, Hosea Carter Sr., and Jack King of Carthage; Kenneth Witcher, Jesse Wood, and Larry J. Tucker of Red Boiling Springs; Lafayette Mayor Page Durham, and James Roark of Lafayette; Gainesboro Mayor Calvin Roark, Brown Meadows, and Donald McCormick of Gainesboro; and Howard Burnley and Willie G. Hogg of Hartsville.

On June 19, the controversy was resolved "temporarily." The directors of the five county anti-poverty program voted to continue to apply funds from the Head Start program to pay Neighborhood Service Center employees. Additionally, the board voted 16-14 not to have an official audit of the Cordell Hull Corporation books.

The official statement from the board indicated that Frieda Biles received authorization from the Atlanta office to use the $52,000 of Head Start funds in question to pay Neighborhood Service Center employees. The Atlanta office was satisfied that there was no improper diversion of OEO funds by the Cordell Hull Corporation.

Biles said that cutbacks imposed by the OEO in 1968 would have necessitated the layoffs of Neighborhood Service Center personnel if the $52,000 hadn't been transferred.

Sources:

"Hull Group Asks Audit." *The Nashville Tennessean*, May 25, 1969.

Korpan, Steve. "Hull Issue Resolved, Audit Dropped." *The Nashville Tennessean*, June 21, 1969.

"Lafayette OEO Probe Opened." *The Nashville Tennessean*, May 16, 1969.

"OEO Officials Deny Hull Funds Probe." *The Nashville Tennessean*, May 17, 1969.

A Stolen Car Ring.

A major auto theft ring had been active in Middle Tennessee for several months. On November 7, District Attorney General Baxter Key said he and the TBI were conducting a thorough investigation into the ring. Key related that as many as 100 vehicles had been stolen by the ring. He added that the TBI had already impounded 17 vehicles.

According to Key the cars had been stolen across the South, brought to Tennessee, given fraudulent registrations, and sold either privately or at car dealerships. Several innocent people, including some in Macon County, had unwittingly purchased the stolen cars.

Suspecting that the ring was getting inside help, Key said he had had seven or eight major suspects, including Tennessee Highway Patrol officer Charles Robinson of Hartsville. The investigation led to Robinson being suspended in mid-December.

His badge, gun, handcuffs, and other gear were confiscated, but he was never arrested.

Sources:

Daughtrey, Larry. "DA Probing Auto Theft Ring." *The Nashville Tennessean*, November 8, 1969.

"Trooper Suspended In Hartsville Probe." *The Nashville Tennessean*, December 15, 1969.

A Civil Rights Violation?

On July 9, a group of Macon County residents filed a suit in federal court seeking an immediate reapportionment of County Court (legislative body) and school board districts. Those filing the class action complaint were Janet Clark, Dr. E. Murrel Froedge, Dr. Frank Bellar, Henry Clay Johnson, Charlie Gregory, and Nelson Hicks. Their attorney, Guy Yelton, said the current apportionment violated the equal protection clause of the 14th Amendment and the "federally protected civil rights of the plaintiffs."

Citing the "one man, one vote" principle, Yelton asked the judge to overrule certain clauses of the Tennessee Constitution and declare them invalid. He based his motion on the fact that some county districts elected more than two magistrates. Yelton pointed out that the Lafayette district elected four magistrates, the Red Boiling Springs district elected three, and all the other districts elected two. Beyond that, according to Yelton, the districts had a wildly disparate number of citizens. For instance, the 8th District had only 2.1% of the county's registered voters while the Lafayette district contained 39.5%.

On December 10, the plaintiffs still represented by Guy Yelton and Macon County represented by James W. Chamberlain faced off in front of U.S. District Judge, William E. Miller. The county presented a reapportionment plan that would consist 15 districts.

There would be two magistrates elected from each district for a total of 30. The five school board members would represent three districts each.

The plaintiffs offered a plan whereby the county would consist of ten districts and twenty magistrates.

The biggest sticking points came when the two sides couldn't agree on the county's population, or even on its physical size. Plaintiff's attorney Yelton told the judge that the county's official population was 14,700. County attorney Chamberlain disagreed with Yelton's estimate. The Chamberlain said it was "more nearly 12,197."

Chamberlain told the judge that the population of Red Boiling Springs was about 590. Red Boiling Springs Mayor Willis Knight testified that he was wasn't sure what the exact population the town was, but he was certain that it was "less than 800."

The physical size of Macon County should have been outside the scope of argument, but it wasn't. Yelton said the county's area was 569 square miles. Chamberlain contended its area was much less than Yelton's estimate. Chamberlain contended that Macon County's size was only 304 square miles.

An exasperated Judge Miller didn't want to rule on the population or physical size of the county without proper information. He ordered the attorneys to return in 45 days with their numbers aligned. They did and Macon County's districts were redrawn in the manner that Chamberlain suggested.

Sources:

"Disagreement Causes Problem in Macon Remap." *The Nashville Tennessean*, December 11, 1969.

Kenyon, Nellie. "Suit Asks Macon Reapportionment." *The Nashville Tennessean*, July 10, 1969.

1970-1971

"Rowdy" Killed.

Every community has its lovable characters. Louis "Rowdy" Haddock was one of Macon County's most lovable characters. Rowdy didn't drive, but he was well-known for his hitchhiking abilities. He could go from town to town in Middle Tennessee very quickly by hitching rides from motorists. However, hitchhiking has always been dangerous.

On April 18, 1970, the 36-year-old Haddock was walking along Highway 25 about one mile east of Hartsville when he was struck by a car. It is possible that with immediate care he may have survived. However, the driver of the car decided to drive on and leave Rowdy to die.

Jimmy Harold Roddy, age 21, was convicted of killing Rowdy and was sentenced to 11 months and 29 days in the Trousdale County Jail. But Roddy's life of violence continued until he died about a year and a half later. On September 16, 1972, Roddy was involved in an altercation un the parking lot of a Hartsville market. The altercation ended with him being shot to death.

According to TBI Agent Frank Evetts and Trousdale County Sheriff Rex Turner, Roddy and a man named Denny White were drinking and they began arguing because Roddy allegedly bumped White's car with a motorcycle. One witness said that only Roddy and White were involved, but two other men may have taken part in the incident. The authorities concluded the White shot Roddy once with a .22-caliber rifle loaded with hollow point bullets. White also struck Roddy over the head several times with a blackjack.

White claimed he acted in self-defense. He told the authorities that Roddy "came at me with a knife and slashed me several times. Agent Evetts and Sheriff Turner described White's injuries as "superficial."

Source:

"Man Convicted of Hit & Run Death of Louis Haddock Dies of Wounds." *The Macon County Times*, September 21, 1972.

"Murfreesboro Death Sends Traffic Toll to 22." *The Nashville Tennessean*, April 20, 1970.

ATF Gets Rid of Gun.

On April 7, 1970, the Alcohol, Tobacco, and Firearms division of the US Treasury Department seized a .38-caliber Smith and Wesson pistol in Macon County. Then, on July 7, Chief Special Investigator, William H. Richardson, gave notice that anyone "claiming an interest" in the weapon could file a claim and pay a $250 bond to get it. Richardson related that if no one filed a claim by August 6, the pistol would be forfeited and would be disposed of according to the law.

Source:

"Department Of The Treasury, Internal Revenue Service." *The Nashville Tennessean*, July 7, 1970.

Another Senseless Shooting.

Billy Waye Swindle was 28. At about 8:45 p.m. on April 22, 1970, he was rushed to the Emergency Room of the hospital at Lafayette. Sadly, he was already dead when he arrived. A few minutes earlier, he had been shot thrice with a .38-caliber pistol. The shooting took place on the Scottsville Road within the Lafayette city limits.

Jackie Pedigo turned himself in to Sheriff Maburn Dyer shortly after the incident. Dyer locked Pedigo in jail, but charges weren't filed immediately.

Source:

"Billy Swindle Shot To Death." *The Macon County Times*, April 23, 1970.

A Prison Break.

On May 16, 1970, two men, one of whom was from Lafayette escaped from the Tennessee state prison in Nashville. Prison Warden, Jim Rose, said the escape happened at about 1:30 a.m. Larry Jones from Lafayette, and another man, Howard Clay Hunter were part of the prison detail assigned to preparing breakfast for the inmates. They overwhelmed dining room steward George White, tied him up, and locked him in a room adjacent to the dining room.

Jones and Hunter didn't injure White, but they took his keys and used them to get themselves out the prison's main entrance located on Centennial Boulevard in West Nashville.

Oddly, even though Jones and Hunter were dressed in their white prison uniforms, guards at the exit didn't see the escapees. It was believed that they scaled the tall, razor wire fence surrounding the prison.

Metro Nashville Police and prison guards used bloodhounds in the search for the escapees. Warden Rose said he didn't think the two convicts were dangerous, but he conceded that they might be armed with a knife.

Jones, who had less than a year remaining on his sentence, went home to his mother's house and waited for the authorities to find him. When they did, he surrendered without incident.

The end came for Larry Jones on September 3, 1985, when he, his teenaged son, and his teenaged nephew were all killed execution style near Hartsville, Tennessee after their attempt to steal a marijuana crop was foiled.

Source:

"Escape State Prison." *The Nashville Tennessean*, May 16, 1970.

Gammon, CL. *Shallow Graves and Shattered Dreams: Solving the Murders of Three Macon County Men*. Lafayette, Tennessee: Deep Read Press, 2021.

Whiskey Raids.

Long after National Prohibition ended, illegal whiskey was still an issue in Tennessee. On August 10, 1971, federal, state, and local officials raided 11 counties mostly in rural Middle Tennessee. Beginning at 4:30 a.m. and working until nightfall, the agents destroyed 222 gallons of illicit liquor, as well as confiscating 18 cars and trucks used to transport the "moonshine."

William Richardson of the ATF said the raids came after months of painstaking investigation. The raids were conducted in Macon, Davidson, Rutherford, Cannon, Fentress, Overton, Clay, DeKalb, Warren, Cumberland, and Pickett counties. In Macon County, James Scruggs was arrested and 7.5 gallons of illegal whiskey found on his property was confiscated.

Source:

"Whiskey Arrests Net 33 Arrests." *The Nashville Tennessean*, August 11, 1971.

1972-1973

Another Slaying.

At about 5 p.m. on March 1, 1972, a shooting took place in City Park in Lafayette. The operating superintendent of Tri-County Electric Membership Corporation, J. T. Keene, age 41, was transported to the hospital in Lafayette. There was no need for the ambulance driver to hurry. Keene was dead.

Keene was survived by his wife Mary and three daughters.

Willie Chesley Parker, age 58, and his son Lonnie Ray Parker, age 36, were held for questioning, but neither was charged immediately.

District Attorney Baxter Key reported that Keene, who had also operated Macon County Hardware, was shot three times with a carbine, and once with a 12-gauge shotgun. Key said, "I understand the weapons belong to the Parkers but we are making a further investigation."

A relative of Keene was also being questioned.

Assistant District Attorney Jackie Bellar, Agent Frank Evetts, of the TBI, and Macon County Sheriff Maburn Dyer were also involved in the investigation.

Key would not comment on the details of the shooting or of any possible motives. However, he did say that the suspected murder weapons were seized.

Source:

"Lafayette Man Slain; Police Question 2." *The Nashville Tennessean*, March 2, 1972.

School Board Lawsuit.

U.S. District Judge L. Clure Morton ruled on June 28, 1972, that a group of Macon County residents were not entitled to a court order mandating the staggering of school board terms. In 1970, after Judge William E. Miller approved a new apportionment plan, the five members of the school board (Melvin Cliburn, B. O. Gammons, Ben Holder, Leon Wooten, and Kenneth Witcher) were elected to six-year terms.

The plaintiffs (Ellis Rader, Jackie Eller, William B. Birdwell, Joel East, and Ray Bilbrey) contended that Miller failed to consider the Tennessee law requiring staggering terms of office. Judge Morton disagreed. His opinion was the "Plaintiffs have failed to provide the court with any proof of any such obvious mistake or oversight."

Morton continued that Miller's plan was "clearly within the discretion of the court."

Source:

"Morton Affirms Non-Staggered Macon Board." *The Nashville Tennessean*, June 29, 1972.

Man Shot to Death.

On July 11, 1972, Orbin Dean Alexander, age 32, of Lafayette died of two gunshot wounds to the chest. He was believed to have been shot near his home with a .32-caliber pistol.

Alexander was survived by his wife, Betty Ruth *Holland* Alexander and two daughters, Audra and Melissa.

James Leon Bullington was taken into custody in connection with the killing, and after a short delay charges were filed against him. Evidently, the shooting occurred as the two men engaged in a heated political argument.

Bullington was convicted of first-degree murder. Unwilling to accept the verdict, Bullington appealed his case all the way to the Tennessee Supreme Court. On January 26, 1976, the High Court turned down Bullington's appeal and upheld his conviction.

Sources:

Hall, Doug. "Judge Return Ordered." *The Nashville Tennessean*, January 27, 1976.

"32 Year Old Macon Man Dies of Gunshot Wound." *The Macon County Times*, July 13, 1972.

Governor Offers Reward.

On the evening of September 26, 1973, the body of Dan P. Smith, a 63-year-old widower from Macon County, was found in a ditch along Highway 52 within the Red Boiling Springs city limits. His death occurred not far from his home. Macon County Sheriff Prentice Patterson and TBI investigators concluded that a hit-and-run driver was responsible for Smith's death.

There had been no break in the case and on February 14, 1974, Governor Winfield's office announced a reward of $1,000 for information leading to the arrest and conviction of the hit-and-run driver.

Source:

"Dunn Offers Reward in Traffic Death" *The Nashville Tennessean*, February 5, 1974.

A Shooting Near the Public Square.

On October 6, 1973, the sound of gunshots ripped through the crisp autumn air. A deadly shooting in the North Central

Telephone Cooperative parking lot left one person dead and two others seriously wounded. 16-year-old Randall Carver opened fire on Floyd Lee Calvert, age 22, of Westmoreland, and brothers Charlie and Ricky Trent of Lafayette. Calvert was transported the few yards to the hospital at Lafayette, where he was pronounced dead on arrival. Charlie, age 20, and Ricky, age 16, were badly hurt and were hospitalized, but both survived.

Witnesses told the authorities that the trio began bullying Carver at the "Old Country Music Barn" just off the Public Square on the Red Boiling Springs Road. The bullying, so said the witnesses, continued at the Sunoco service station on the Public Square. Then, the shooting event happened in the North Central parking lot a few minutes later.

After the shooting, Carver went to the Macon County jail, just off the Public Square with some of his friends and he surrendered there.

City Police Officers Larry Cole, Reed Long, and Ronald Parker, along with Sheriff Prentice Patterson and Constable Lyn Shrum investigated the shooting.

Source:

"Saturday Night Shooting By Juvenile Leaves One Dead, Two Seriously Wounded." *The Macon County Times*, October 11, 1973.

1974-1975

A Failed Appeal.

On May 20, 1974, the Tennessee Court of Criminal Appeals upheld the convictions of Newman Robinson and his son Mark. The men were convicted of petty larceny for the alleged theft of a radiator from a Macon County garage and sentenced to serve six months in the Macon County jail. The Robinsons appealed on the grounds that Macon County Sheriff Prentice Patterson was outside his jurisdiction when he took them into custody.

Source:

"Court Orders Hearing for Man Convicted of Murder." *The Nashville Tennessean*, May 21, 1974.

Lady Bank Robbers.

The search for a bank robbery team from Kentucky spilled over into Macon County on August 8, 1974.

About 10:15 a.m. two bandits held up the Holland Branch of the Scottsville, Kentucky National Bank, took about $12,000, then sped away in a blue 1974 Maverick, going south toward Tennessee.

Bank teller Bruce W. Gibbs reported the robbery. He said two women pulled the bank job. One of them sported an automatic pistol and the other one handed him a note saying, "We're here for a withdrawal, and we want the money quick."

The authorities weren't interested in the fact that it was the bank teller's birthday. It was certainly a birthday he'd never forget.

That evening, Macon County Sheriff Prentice Patterson stated, "We've had reports that that the (getaway) car was seen in the area near the Sumner County line, and believe it is hidden in the woods."

The suspected bank robbers didn't stay at large for long. They were arrested in Nashville at about 6 p.m. on August 9. The suspects were identified as Sherry J. Paris, age 30, of Nashville and Margaret Francis Sullivan, age 27, of Westmoreland. Paris was a licensed practical nurse and Sullivan was unemployed. Paris was identified as the bank robber who flashed the automatic pistol. If convicted, the women stood to receive up to 25 years in prison and be and liable for a fine of $10,000 each.

FBI agent Thomas W. Kitchens Jr. offered high praise for the various police departments involved in the investigation. He said an "intensive and cooperative" investigation involving Kentucky State police, the Allen County, Kentucky, and Macon County, Sheriff's Departments developed information that led to the arrests.

The only remaining question concerned the stolen money. Some of the money was recovered at the time of the arrest, but "a substantial amount" was unaccounted for.

Sources:

Hall, Doug. "Two Women Held as Bank Rob Suspects." *The Nashville Tennessean*, August 11, 1974.

Reed, Alan R. "Woman Bank Bandit Search Enters State." *The Nashville Tennessean*, August 9, 1974.

Tobacco Thieves.

Raymond Jones of Gallatin, age 31, and his father, C.C. Jones of Castalian Springs, age 62, were in loads of trouble. On May 8, 1975, Raymond was found guilty in Sumner County of concealing stolen property. He was given a sentence of 3-5 years. But that was just the beginning. He and his father still faced charges in Sumner County of concealing stolen truck bodies and felonious possession of explosives.

Beyond all that, they were scheduled to stand trial in Macon County in June for stealing a truck loaded with tobacco.

Source:

"Sumner Jury Deals Man 3-5 Years On $750 Stolen Rifle Charges." *The Nashville Tennessean*, May 9, 1975.

Missing Money.

State Comptroller, William Snodgrass, stated on August 21, 1975, that he had found $505,381 in shortages in 130 county offices across Tennessee between 1968 and 1973. However, only five people had been charged and only three people had been convicted in connection with the shortages.

Snodgrass explained the reasons for the lack of convictions were twofold. First, District Attorney Generals didn't usually prosecute offenders if the offenders reimbursed their counties. Secondly, there was usually no criminal intent involved with the shortages.

There were a few shortages in Macon County offices. The state made no allegations of criminal intent of any person in the Macon County government and the county was reimbursed for all the shortages found.

The shortages Snodgrass found in Macon County included:

Fiscal Year 1968-1969: Trustee's Office, $543.39.
Fiscal Year 1969-1970: Trustee's Office, $2,839.29.
Fiscal Year 1970-1971: County Court Clerk's Office, $1,608.
Fiscal Year 1972-1973: Trustee's Office, $704.61.

Source:

Sutherland, Frank. "5 of 130 Officials Tried for Shortages." *The Nashville Tennessean*, August 22, 1975.

Fireman Charged with Arson.

Danny Newberry, age 21, had been training with the Lafayette Volunteer Fire Department, but he wasn't destined to become a member of that important organization.

On September 19, 1975, he was arrested and charged with three counts of arson. Newberry actually helped fight the fires he was accused of setting. Newberry was jailed and held in lieu of $50,000 bond.

Newberry, a full-time body shop employee, allegedly set fire to three establishments over a period of five days:

1. September 3: the Macon County Livestock Market. The fire caused an estimated $60,000 in damage and killed 130 head of cattle.
2. September 6: The Smith Brothers Feed Mill.
3. September 8: Carr Brothers Farm Supplies.

Luckily, no one was injured or killed in any of the fires Newberry was accused of starting.

Lafayette Chief of Police, Norman Farley, arrested Newberry after Volunteer Fireman, J. H. Dallas, brought the suspect to the police station. Dallas had been investigating the rash of fires in the city on his own and he confronted Newberry about them on the previous evening.

Newberry had been assisting the Volunteer Fire Department but he had not been made an official member. One became a member after going through training and then being elected by a vote of the other volunteer firemen. Full-fledged members received $5 for each fire they fought within the Lafayette city limits.

There had been ten local fires attributed to arson in recent weeks and a local businessman had offered $10,000 for the arrest and conviction of the culprits. The authorities could only tie Newberry to three of the fires.

Newberry's preliminary hearing was before General Sessions Judge Doyle Jenkins on September 26.

Source:

"Fireman Trainee Charged With Arson." *The Nashville Tennessean*, September 21, 1975.

A Sunshine Law Violation?

Former Supervisor of the Macon County Ambulance Service Charles F. Thompson filed suit in Chancery Court on September 21, 1975. Thompson alleged that the County Court Committee that replaced him violated the Tennessee Sunshine Law in the process.

The Sunshine Law mandated that government agencies were bound to hold their meetings in full public view.

It was Thompson's contention that the Ambulance Committee violated the law during its "emergency meeting" on July 14. It was at that meeting that the committee replaced Thompson with Alvin Chitwood.

Thompson further claimed that there was no reason for the "emergency meeting" to be held; that the public was barred from the session; that no public notice of the meeting was given beforehand; and no record of the individual votes was entered into the minutes of the meeting.

Thompson held that the committee, County Judge Aubrey Dallas, and the Quarterly Court "were intentional and without cause and that actions taken by the committee in its unlawful 'emergency' session should be declared void and of no effect."

James B. Dance was Thompson's attorney. Dance asked that the judge permanently enjoin the County Court from violating the Sunshine Law and that the Chancery Court maintain jurisdiction over "the parties and subject matter" for one year "from the date of entry."

Dance conceded that the County Court had the authority to allow the 5-member Ambulance Committee to hire personnel. But he held that because the committee meeting was at variance with the law, the actions of July 14 couldn't take effect.

Source:

"Sunshine Law Violation Charged." *The Nashville Tennessean*, September 22, 1975.

1976-1977

Hiding a Sports Car.

A federal grand jury indicted Macon County insurance salesman Bobby Gene Jenkins on February 18, 1976. He was accused of receiving and concealing a stolen 1975 Chevrolet Carmaro which had been moved in interstate commerce.

During the days of John Dillinger, Bonnie and Clyde, and other Depression era gangsters, Congress adopted a bill making car theft such as the one Jenkins was alleged to be involved with a federal crime. If convicted, Jenkins could receive up to five years in prison and be fined up to $5,000.

Source:

Vandeberg, Marsha. "Brentwood Minister Faces Charge to Defraud Church Investors." *The Nashville Tennessean*, February 19, 1976.

An Entire Family Killed.

At about 2 a.m. on March 1, 1976, a terribly horrible event took place. A husband, his wife, and their three children were all shot to death. Macon County Deputy Ray Chandler identified the victims as Charles Mayhew, age 48; Jean Mayhew; Judy Mayhew, age 13; Diane Mayhew, age 11; and Steve Mayhew, age 6.

The Mayhews lived in a mobile home about nine miles from Lafayette. Charles was a retired veteran of the Merchant Marine Corps who was disabled from heart disease. He was believed to be from Michigan or Indiana.

Jean Mayhew was employed at a Hartsville nursing home.

Deputy Chandler said there was no sign of struggle in the mobile home. This and other factors led him, the other deputies who viewed the scene, and TBI agent Don Clark to conclude that they were looking at a murder-suicide. They surmised that Charles Mayhew had shot his wife and children with a .22-caliber rifle. Then, he put the rifle barrel in his mouth and pulled the trigger.

Investigators found Jean in her bed. Judy and Diane were in another bedroom in their bunk beds. Steve was lying on the living room couch. He was shot between the eyes.

A Mayhew neighbor named Betty Shrum discovered the gruesome scene. Concerned about the family, Shrum went to mobile home at about 6:30 p.m. on the day of the shooting. She peered through an opening in the front door and saw Steve's blood splattered body lying the couch. There was no question that the child was dead.

Sheriff Department dispatcher Stanley Massey went to the scene with the deputies. Shocked, he said, "It was the grimmest thing I ever saw. I don't know why something like this would happen.

Source:

"Macon County Family of Five Shot to Death." *The Nashville Tennessean*, March 2, 1976.

A Big Pot Bust.

On July 31, 1976, Macon County Sheriff Hollis McClard and seven deputies engaged in a major drug raid in the northwestern section of the county. They took Nashvillian Frank Dowling Flitcroft, age 28, into custody.

Extremely proud of their work, McClard said he and his team confiscated marijuana and other drugs worth "several thousand dollars." But he didn't put an exact value on the drugs he found. In all, according to McClard, the raid netted 17 pounds of marijuana, about 10 pounds of marijuana seeds, and 13 bottles of "small white pills." Sheriff McClard stated, "We're going to send samples of everything to the toxicology lab for a formal analysis."

McClard commented that he believed Flitcroft was running a professional operation. He pointed out that the marijuana and seeds were "all packaged up in plastic bags for sale."

Authorities officially charged Flitcroft with "possession of more than one-half ounce of marijuana" and lodged him in the Macon County jail in lieu of a $50,000 bail.

Source:

"Nashvillian Jailed In Macon Pot Case." *The Nashville Tennessean*, August 2, 1976.

A Conflict of Interest?

A state audit released of December 2, 1976, found that board members of the Upper Cumberland Development District had an "apparent conflict of interest" in the financial activities of the organization. The auditor contended that members of the Upper Cumberland Development Board of Directors were also board members the Upper Cumberland Development Corporation. Most of those mentioned were also political leaders within their home counties.

The alleged conflict of interest was found in the fact that the corporation received rent payments from the development district. State Comptroller William Snodgrass recommended the dissolution of the corporation, but the board members rejected the idea. The consensus was that the board members did not profit from the rent payments and that no crimes had been committed.

Macon County Judge Aubrey Dallas was one of those that was serving on the boards of both organizations.

Source:

Sutherland, Frank. "Cumberland Money Conflict Seen." *The Nashville Tennessean*, December 3, 1976.

Executives Indicted.

On November 14, 1977, a grand jury handed down several indictments against Genesco Executives accused of defrauding the company. Billy Rhea Flynn, who served as Vice President of the Genesco manufacturing division until he was fired on December 8, 1975, was indicted on 14-counts. Along with Flynn, Alfred Turner was indicted. Turner had served as manager of the Harpeth Apparel Plant in Red Boiling Springs until February 10, 1977, when he was fired.

The two were accused of defrauding Genesco by inflating billing invoices for the washing of blue jeans at laundries they set up. According to the indictment, Flynn and Turner set up Hudson's Laundry in Red Boiling Springs and another laundry in Kentucky and charged Genesco $87,278.58 for laundering blue jeans and then split the profits.

Flynn denied any wrongdoing. He said, "I feel without a doubt that I will prove my innocence. My attorneys believe I will prove my innocence. I will do everything I can to clear myself." While he said his actions were "completely proper," Flynn didn't go into details.

Source:

Hall, Doug. "3 Genesco, 1 Loan Exec Indicted." *The Nashville Tennessean*, November 15, 1977.

1978-1979

A Hit-and-Run Death.

On Sept 11, 1978, at about 7:30 p.m. a tragedy occurred. Barbara Pryor and her two young sons, David Eugene, age 4, and William Ray, age 6, walking across the Westmoreland Road at the Brattontown community in Macon County. As they crossed the road, Kent J. Day allegedly struck Barbara and David with his car and drove on. Barbara suffered a broken leg and David was killed.

The authorities later arrested Day. Charged him with "leaving the scene of an accident involving bodily harm, driving with a revoked license, and vehicular homicide by doing bodily damage with an automobile to a person." Day was lodged in the Macon County Jail in lieu of a $25,000 bond.

Source:

Witcher, Russ. "Man Jailed in Hit-Run Death." *The Nashville Tennessean*, September 18, 1978.

A Liquor Store Robbery.

Northgate Liquors in Hartsville had a large amount of cash on hand at 3 p.m. on February 8, 1979. The reason for the register brimming with cash was, according to Hartsville Police Officer Ronnie Earps, because it was payday at the Hartsville Nuclear Plant construction site.

Perhaps a group of thieves from Nashville knew that the liquor store had more cash than on other days, or maybe they just got "lucky." Regardless, one criminal kept the clerk occupied in the wine section while another one emptied the register. Then the two men were joined by two women outside the liquor store, jumped into their car, and streaked to the north.

The robbers absconded with between $10,000 and $15,000, in cash but it did them no good. Alert authorities in Macon County quickly arrested three of the four criminals near a Red Boiling Spring eatery. The fourth was caught later running in the frozen snow nearby.

The most important thing to Trousdale County Sheriff Charles Robinson was that the robbers were in custody, but he was troubled by the fact that only $820 of the stolen money had been recovered. According to Robinson, the robbers threw their loot out the window of their car while they were being pursued by the police near Red Boiling Springs. Most of the money was evidently scattered and buried under six inches of snow.

Sources:

Highers, Martha, "Hartsville Liquor Store Robbery Nets 3 Arrests: Suspect Sought." *The Nashville Tennessean*, February 9, 1979.

Highers, Martha, "3 Robbery Suspects Identified." *The Nashville Tennessean*, February 11, 1979.

Big Drug Round Up.

On April 25, 1979, law enforcement officers in Wilson, Smith, Trousdale and Macon counties began a roundup of nearly 100 alleged drug dealers in Middle Tennessee. The raids were the result of an undercover operation of about six months.

District Attorney General Tommy Thompson said that various grand juries had returned "140 indictments against more than 90 individuals who sold drugs to our agents." Thompson said that bond for the marijuana dealers would be set at $2,500 and those accused of selling "hard drugs" would have their bonds set at $5,000.

All the raids except one began at 6 p.m. and involved officers from all four counties, the TBI, and the Tennessee Highway Patrol. The one arrest that happened before 6 p.m. was that of Chris Wright, age 18, of Lebanon. According to Terry Ashe, Wright had a job after school somewhere in Nashville and we didn't want him to get out of pocket."

The biggest fish in the raids was, according to Thompson, a Macon County man named William Dixon. Thompson believed the 29-year-old Dixon was "a major supplier for marijuana and pills throughout several of our counties."

Warrant in hand, District Attorney Thompson and a dozen officers raided Dixon's beautiful home in rural Macon County. The officers arrested Dixon outside his home, but a pretty blonde-haired woman named Debbie Wix locked the doors to the house and refused to allow anyone enter for several minutes. Wix was alleged to be living with Dixon.

After trying to get Wix open the door for several minutes, one officer was out of patience. He yelled to Wix, "I'm going to kick this damned door in right now if you don't open up." At that point, Dixon offered to open the door with the house keys he had in his pants pocket. Once inside the house, the lawmen realized that they had taken Dixon and Wix by such surprise that dinner was still cooking on the stove.

Lafayette Chief of Police Buford Wix and Debbie Wix were related by marriage, but that didn't stop him from placing her under arrest. He began reading her rights to her, but she interrupted him. She asked, "What is this for?"

The Chief answered curtly, "Selling durgs."

"I ain't sold any drugs," she shot back.

Chief Wix continued reading her rights to her.

The search of Dixon's home turned up a stash of 2.5 pounds of marijuana, a selection of suspected narcotics and $5,000 in cash.

Thompson said 25 were indicted in Macon County, but he only named 10 of those arrested on the first day. He said those taken into custody in Macon County were Jimmy Andrews, Donald C.

Reid, Johnny Coley, Larry Mitchell, Ricky Harp, Don Smith, Terry Wooten, Travis Bean, Rivky Gregory, Mark Shelton, Debbie Wix, and William Dixon.

As of April 26, only about eight of the 90 alleged drug pushers were still at large. District Attorney Thompson said some of those indicted might not be found, because some of the transactions took place back in October and November."

The grand juries heard from two informants who worked undercover for the authorities. Thompson said, "We had a third, but she fell in love with one of the drug dealers and didn't stay in the program very long."

Officers said on April that 22 of the 25 alleged drug dealers indicted in Macon County had been arrested, but they didn't release any new names.

Source:

Gregory, Ed. "Drug Roundup Believed Big Success." *The Nashville Tennessean*, April 27, 1979.

Gregory, Ed. "4 Counties Begin Drug Round-Up." *The Nashville Tennessean*, April 26, 1979.

A True Mystery.

On July 24, 1979, a man was spotted wandering aimlessly along a lonely road in Macon County. The unshaven man had brown hair and deep brown eyes. He was slender, standing 5-10 and weighing 140 pounds. He appeared to be more than 40 years old. His outstanding physical feature was a deep scar on his forehead.

The man had no identification. In fact, all he was carrying was $1.31 in cash, and a cardboard box containing three pairs of double-knit pants, and one pair of "uniform" pants "like a Texaco serviceman would wear," four short sleeve shirts and one long sleeve shirt. The box didn't contain any socks or underwear.

Macon County Deputies picked up the clearly disoriented man and took him to the county jail for questioning. They asked the man questions for several minutes but he didn't respond. All they learned about him was that he was a chain smoker.

With nothing to hold him on, the deputies put the man in a patrol car, drove him down Highway 10 to the Trousdale County line, put him out, and drove away. But the mystery man didn't walk on toward Hartsville. Instead, he walked back up the hill toward Lafayette.

About 6:30 a.m. on July 25, Lafayette City Policeman James "Dude" Harper saw the mystery man "prowling" in the patrol car in the driveway. It was later presumed that the man was looking for cigarettes. Harper took the man to the police station and officers tried to question him. But again, the man didn't provide any answers. Sometimes he would nod or shake his head, but his responses had no relation to the questions officers were asking him. Chief Buford Wix said that despite being non-responsive, the man "seemed to understand what I'm saying."

At last, the man took a pen and scrawled the words "Ellie Murphee" on a sheet of paper. The words meant nothing to the officers.

Unable to help the mystery man, the authorities transferred him to the Plateau Mental Health Center at Cookeville. The hope that the mental health professionals there could solve the mystery, or failing that, could at least provide for his needs.

Source:

Highers, Martha, "Mystery Man's Only Clue: Scribbled 'Ellie Murphee.'" *The Nashville Tennessean*, August 9, 1979.

Fix the Jail or Shut it Down.

On November 6, 1979, the state inspected the Macon County Jail and found it violated state safety standards and that it should either be renovated, expanded, or closed. The inspector found that there were no written plans for dealing with emergencies such as escapes, prisoner disturbances, or assaults on employees. There were no emergency evacuation plans either.

The inspection also found that there was inadequate square footage in the cell areas and the plumbing was substandard. Additionally, the inspection pointed out ten lesser deficiencies.

The report on the inspection, which wasn't issued until February 17, 1980, irritated County Judge Aubrey Dallas. He asked, "A few years ago we were in the top seven or eight among the county jails in the state, where were you then?" Dallas continued, "We just renovated our jail a few years ago."

Macon County Sheriff Rex Gann agreed that the jail had been renovated in 1976, but he admitted that there were things that should have been done but weren't. Gann said, "The jail is just too small for the traffic we've had in her the last couple of years. We need a separate cellblock area for women and juveniles, and we don't have that now."

Gann's wish list also included a security fence so the inmates could go out into the sunshine occasionally. Gann said, "Right now, there are no windows upstairs where the men are kept."

Source:

Lewis, Dwight. "Report: Upgrade Or Shut Down 3 County Jails." *The Nashville Tennessean*, February 18, 1980.

1980-1981

Polluter Fined.

On July 18, 1980, the Tennessee Water Quality Control agency announced it was seeking a $70,000 assessment against Mid-South Stone, Inc. for polluting two streams near the company's Macon County quarry. Mid-South Stone, a subsidiary of Mid-South Paving Inc. of Nashville, was charged with seven violations of the Water Quality Control Act. Each violation carried a fine of $10,000. The allegations were that the company discharged by-products of its operation into Goose Creek and Carter Branch in Macon County.

An attorney for the Tennessee Public Health Department's Division of Water Quality Control said that "fine material, like sand" was flowing away from the quarry site into the streams. He said the company also polluted Goose Creek when it "pushed some material into the stream in building a bridge."

Mid-South Stone contested the state's allegations. Its safety director and environmental manager was Scott B. Witherspoon. Witherspoon said, "They (the state) claim such a large amount (of limestone) was harmful to marine life, but limestone itself is not a pollutant." Witherspoon continued that procedures at the Macon County quarry had "completely changed" since the alleged violations occurred nine months earlier. Witherspoon called the fines "unjust" and promised, "We're going to fight it to the hilt."

However, Mid-South Stone's attorney stated that the company might not contest the fines at all. He said, "The decision has not been made. We are in the process of initiating discussions with the state about the matter."

As is often the case, a compromise was found. Mid-South Stone avoided paying most of the $70,000 fine. The parties agreed that the company would be assessed $6,000 ($1,000 for each of six violations). The company had informed the state of its efforts to purify the water it polluted in the two streams. A spokesman for the state said, "We have discussed the problem with the company. They convinced us that they had paid considerable sums of money to clear up the problem, and the problem no longer exists."

One charge was dropped completely because it involved the building of an unauthorized bridge across Goose Creek. Mis-South Stone proved that its wasn't liable because the previous owners of the quarry built the bridge.

Mid-South Stone accepted the state's decision and paid the fine.

Sources:

Hall, Alan. "Firm Assessed $6,000 for Polluting." *The Nashville Tennessean*, August 23, 1980.

$70,000 Pollution Damages Sought in Macon Creek Case." *The Nashville Tennessean*, July 9, 1980.

A Christmas Eve Murder.

Christmas 1980 wasn't merry for the family of Stanley E. Kemp. About noon on Christmas Eve, the body of the 25-year-old Macon County man was found in a barn near Burkesville, Kentucky. He was under a pile of burning tobacco sticks.

Kemp had been dead 10 to 12 hours before he was found. He had been burning for more than three hours before being discovered. A group of people passed the barn and saw smoke coming from it at about 9 a.m. They didn't investigate because they surmised that someone was inside stripping tobacco. As mentioned earlier, Kemp wasn't found until around noon.

Macon County Sheriff, Rex Gann, conducted the investigation into the case. Gann said that Kemp had a "crippled" arm and leg, but despite his disability, he worked with the Macon County

Highway Department. Kemp had received his weekly pay check on December 23 and was last seen later that evening at a tavern in Carthage with an unknown man.

The sheriff said the murderers "were trying to burn the barn down and were hoping the body would be burned beyond recognition so nobody in Kentucky would be able to identify him. We're pulling people in to see if we can get a correct lead on the people who were with the subject the night before."

Gann continued, "We're still trying to find out who all he was with Saturday night. We have been able to place him in two different cars at 8 p.m., but that's about all I would want to say about that right now."

Gann did comment on other things, however. The autopsy found that Kemp was killed by a blow to the top of the head caused by a blunt object. The sheriff stated that Kemp "had cuts on his head like he was hit with a pipe." Gann related that a pipe was found in the barn.

Gann believed that robbery was the likely motive.

Roger Sampson, a Macon County resident, was indicted for the crime in March of 1981. Then, on March 20, 1982, after a trial of two days, a Burkesville jury deliberated for three hours before finding Sampson guilty. The jury recommended that he serve 20 years in prison.

Source:

"Guilty Verdict Reached In Kentucky Murder." *The Nashville Tennessean*, March 21, 1982.

"3 Suspects Sought In Slaying of Man." *The Nashville Tennessean*, December 30, 1980.

Blanton Bid-Rigging.

A federal grand jury was called to investigate bid-rigging in Tennessee. Subjects in the schemes to obtain road building contracts at inflated prices included former Governor Ray Blanton's brother Gene and his uncle Jake. The grand jury was especially interested in projects that were awarded in Macon and Putnam while Ray Blanton was still in office. The low bid for the Macon County project was $3.3 million.

FBI agent John Gisler testified on February 13, 1981, that Gene Blanton convinced Shelbyville contractors Gerald and Joe Tillett to bid on the Macon County project and not bid on a contract in Putnam County. Gisler told the grand jury, "The Tillett brothers acquiesced after assurances by Gene Blanton that he would assist them in rigging" the Macon County contract "if the Tillett brothers ran into any trouble. Telephone conversations occurred between Gene Blanton and the Tillett brothers concerning what contract the Tillett brothers were going to bid during the letting."

At the time of Gisler's testimony, the Tillett brothers were serving four months each in jail for rigging the Macon County project.

A few days after Gisler's testimony, Gene and Jake Blanton were indicted for helping rig the bids on the Macon County project. The indictment charged that before the state deadline of October 20, 1978, an agreement was reached among the conspirators that the Tillett brothers would get the Macon County contract and Hubbs Construction Company would get the Putnam County contract. Then, according to the indictment, the conspirators "agreed to submit, and submitted fraudulent, collusive, noncompetitive, and rigged bids which were intentionally higher in total dollars" than the companies that were designated to receive the contracts.

On April 6, 1981, Jake Blanton entered a plea of guilty to the charge of conspiring to rig the bidding process for the Macon County contract.

Sources:

Clurman, Carol. "Bid-Rig Panel Said Studying 2 Blanton Kin." *The Nashville Tennessean*, February 14, 1981.

Clurman, Carol. "Gene, Jake Blanton Himself Guilty of Bid-Rigging, Admits Associate." *The Nashville Tennessean*, February 19, 1981.

Clurman, Carol. "Jake Blanton Set to Plead Guilty Today." *The Nashville Tennessean*, April 6, 1981.

Crowe, Adell and Joel Kaplan. "60 names Bared in Blanton Bid-Rig Probe." *The Nashville Tennessean*, March 23, 1981.

Sexual Misconduct.

The Trial of Jim R. Burrow, of Lafayette was to get underway on June 19, 1981, in Gallatin. Burrow, a former probation officer, was accused of soliciting sexual favors from his female clients. He was indicted on 11 counts of official oppression and two counts of solicitation of prostitution.

Jury selection was set to begin at 9 a.m. and District Attorney General Roy Whitley felt, "The whole trial will probably be completed in one day. I don't think it will go beyond that." The District Attorney expected to call six of Burrow's female clients as well as TBI agents Jim Taylor and Sam Reece.

Taylor said the investigation began on February 11, 1981, when two women complained about Burrow's actions toward them.

Taylor said he equipped four of Burrow's clients with hidden microphones and they spoke to Burrow at the Sumner County Court House and the Sumner County jail. Tape recordings of the encounters between Burrow and his clients allegedly proved that he "fondled some of them, made sexual innuendoes toward others and asked two of them to work as prostitutes, giving him half their profits."

Taylor identified the female voices on the tapes as those of Crystal Johnson, Joni Brown Sullivan, Janet Dawn Moore, and Rhonda Dixon.

Taylor stated that one of the tapes contained a promise by Burrow to a client "that if she would go to bed with him, he'd guarantee her probation," even though she hadn't gone to trial yet.

Taylor continued that Burrow allegedly told a parolee that he would not help her regain custody of her child unless she slept with him.

The 13 charges against Burrow were all misdemeanors, but he could receive a sentence of up to 11 months and 29 days on each count.

Burrow's attorney said the trial could last more than one day, "depending on how many witnesses the state calls." The truth was that the lawyer didn't want a full-blown trial at all. Burrow admitted his guilt to six of the charges against him, and the District Attorney dropped the other seven charges. The judge sentenced Burrow to six months in jail and ordered him to pay a $1,000 fine.

Burrow's attorney believed he could get the judge to suspend the jail time. The lawyer said he'd call character witnesses in support of his client.

Sources:

"Ex Parole Officer Gets Term on Sex Charges." *The Knoxville News-Sentinel*, June 321, 1981.

Highers, Michael. "Ex-Probation Officer Draws Six-month Term." *The Nashville Tennessean*, June 20, 1981.

Highers, Michael. "Ex-Probation Officer's Trial On Sex Counts Begins Today." *The Nashville Tennessean*, June 19, 1981.

Sears Driver's Theft.

A Nashville truck driver named Curtis E. Westmoreland was arrested for theft a second time on August 7, 1981. Westmoreland was accused of stealing approximately $450,000 in merchandise from his employer of 17 years, Sears Roebuck and Company.

TBI agent Jim Taylor said authorities had recovered between $16,000 and $20,000 in merchandise stolen from Macon and Sumner counties. He continued, "The investigation in Macon County is still being conducted."

Westmoreland was, if nothing else, blatant in turning the stolen merchandise into cash. He sold stolen goods such as microwaves and sewing machines directly out of the back of his Sears delivery truck.

Source:

"Driver Arrested Again On New Theft Charges." *The Nashville Tennessean*, August 8, 1981.

1982-1984

Election Contests.

The 1982 Republican primaries in Macon County on May 4, resulted in some hard feelings and a couple of protests. Two incumbents who lost in the official tallies filed official complaints with the Tennessee Republican Primary Board.

Sheriff Rex Gann finished 1,190 votes behind challenger Bill Music, but he filed an official Notice of Election Contest on May 12. The notice stated that Music, or his supporters, registered a Jackson County resident to vote in Macon County. The notice included a statement from a man living in Jackson County. He said his "mentally retarded" son, also a resident of Jackson County, was registered to vote in Maxon County and that the man voted in the primary.

Gann contended that Music, or his supporters, made promises of jobs in exchange for votes. Gann's complaint also charged that residents of Sumner County, Clay County, and the state of Indiana were permitted to vote in the primary. Gann did not list the names of those he claimed voted illegally.

Fred Steen, seeking his third term as Circuit Court Clerk finished behind Glenn Harold Donoho in the official tabulation 2,194 to 2,183. Steen filed a Notice of Election Contest seeking to overturn Donoho's 11 vote victory. Steen's complaint contended that officials failed to count five votes cast for him in the 10th district and counted one vote for Donoho that should have not been counted. Steen also held that election officials allowed 13 convicted felons to vote illegally. Steen listed the names of the 13 he claimed voted illegally.

The Tennessee Primary Board met on June 1 an, as almost always happens in such cases, allowed the official results to stand.

Music defeated his Democratic opponent in the General Election and Donoho ran unopposed.

Source:

Fisher, Kitty. "2 Contesting Macon Vote After Losing." *The Nashville Tennessean,* May 20, 1982.

No Macon Bridge for Trousdale.

The office of Tennessee Attorney General William M. Leech issued an opinion on June 7, 1982, that Trousdale County could not legally secure the right of way for the Middle Fork bridge in Macon County. Trousdale County Executive C. K. Smith said, "For some reason, a few years ago, right away was given to Trousdale County by Macon County for maintenance of the bridge." Smith then continued, "Trousdale County recently received an 80% federal grant to work on bridges in this county. We would have to put up 20%."

Smith wrote Leech's office asking if Trousdale County could get the Tennessee legislature to adjust the Trousdale and Macon County lines just enough to put the Middle Fork bridge in Trousdale County where the grant money could be used to maintain it.

The Attorney's office replied that the Tennessee Constitution prohibited the physical reduction of any county that was already smaller than 500 square miles and that Macon County was well below the 500 square miles threshold.

Smith wanted to find a solution. The Middle Fork bridge needed to be maintained because it served a road in Trousdale County. Smith said, "I have written Judge (Aubrey) Dallas in Macon County explaining the response of the attorney's office. We will be willing to work out a possible arrangement whereby Macon County could come up with the 20% of the money and we could give them the 80%. We could even work out an arrangement where we would trade off. The bottom line is Trousdale County money cannot be spent on Macon County roads."

The Trousdale County Commission continued to look for ways to solve the Middle Fork bridge problem. On July 26, the Commission voted to continue to explore the construction of a new bridge at Middle Fork.

Sources:

West, Jane, "'Can't Annex Macon Bridge,' Trousdale Told." *The Nashville Tennessean*, June 8, 1982.

West, Jane, "Despite Cut, Tax Bills to Increase." *The Nashville Tennessean*, July 27, 1982.

County Official Accused of Fraud.

Former Macon County Road Supervisor Jack Goodman went on trial at Cookeville on July 9, 1982. He was charged with 38 counts mail fraud in connection with kickbacks he allegedly took from chemical supply companies.

A federal grand jury indicted Goodman in April 1982 on charges that between December 1976 and October 1979, he obtained money from Macon County through payments the county made to Mistoc Supply Company and Two-States Chemical Supply Company. James Sidney Rose owned companies. Rose had been convicted in 1981 of paying kickbacks to a Henry County Road Supervisor and to 18 judges in Arkansas.

The case against Goodman centered on 38 checks paid to Rose's companies by Macon County. The total amount involved was nearly $19,000. Prosecutors claimed that Rose and Goodman split the money from those checks between themselves.

At trial, prosecutors alleged that Rose paid Goodman $100 to $150 on the five shipments of fuel additives Rose's companies delivered to Macon County. The prosecutors claimed that 33 shipments were never received and that Rose and Goodman pocketed the money Macon County paid for them. If convicted, on all 38 counts, Goodman could get a prison term of up to 190 years and be levied a fine of up to $38,000.

Rose was one of the first witnesses in the case, but his testimony apparently didn't damage the defense very much. Goodman took the stand too. He testified that he had never received any money from the alleged scheme.

The case went to the jury on the afternoon of July 10. Then, after only 3.5 hours of deliberation, the jury foreman reported that the panel was hopeless deadlocked. Judge L. Clure Morton declared a mistrial and said he schedule a second trial for "July or August."

The new trial took place in mid-August and the jury began deliberations on August 17. The jury was out a brief time before acquitting Goodman on all 38 counts.

Sources:

"Ex-Road Official's Fraud Trial Begins." *The Nashville Tennessean*, July 10, 1982.

"Jury Hung in Macon County Road Chief's Fraud Trial." *The Nashville Tennessean*, July 11, 1982.

Morgan, Jeri. "U.S. Jury Clears Macon Official of Mail Fraud." *The Nashville Tennessean*, August 18, 1982.

Honeymooner Sent to Jail.

Billy Jennings, age 35, was enjoying his honeymoon on the afternoon of April 18, 1983. Then he decided to go into a Lebanon convenience store and pick up a six-pack of beer. Jennings was an unlucky man that day.

District Attorney General Tommy Thompson just happened to be in the store too. Thompson recognized Jennings as a wanted criminal and he alerted the authorities. Jennings was soon back in prison.

Truthfully, it is possible that Jennings didn't know he was a fugitive. He had entered a guilty plea on two counts of second-degree burglary in Wilson County in September of 1982, and received a prison term of 3-5 years. Jennings had previously been convicted in Macon County on a charge of receiving and concealing stolen property. He received a sentence of 1-3 years for that crime. However, he remained free until his probation was revoked in January 1982.

Jennings was supposed to serve his sentences from Macon County and Wilson County consecutively, but there was a snafu. Prison officials released him from custody on April 14, 1983 thinking wrongly that his Macon County conviction had been suspended.

Jennings had used his four days of freedom to take a bride and embark on a honeymoon.

Source:

"Buying Beer on Honeymoon Puts Convicted Burglar Back in Prison." *The Nashville Tennessean*, April 19, 1983.

A Case of Special Treatment?

On April 27, 1983, Larry Wix, age 29, the son of State Representative Mayo Wix, was suspended from his job for 30 days. The younger Wix, a state motor vehicle investigator for the Tennessee Department of Revenue, had been involved in a shooting while off duty. Allegedly, the Macon County Sheriff's Department under Bill Music "hushed up" the affair.

The incident occurred at about 7 p.m. on March 9, 1983, in Macon County's Rocky Mound community. Larry Wix allegedly engaged in an alteration with a man about the man's estranged wife. During the alteration, Wix, who was said to be drunk, fired the handgun that had been issued to him by the Department of Revenue. No one was injured.

Russ Tipton, chief of motor vehicle investigations in Tennessee said, "I was advised that the Macon County deputies did not take any action due to fact that investigator Wix was intoxicated. If the afore mentioned allegations were proven by a full investigation, investigator Wix should be fired. However, due to other law enforcement agencies' involvement and their reluctance to participate in a comprehensive investigation, voicing their strong desire not to be involved, I request that investigator Wix be suspended for 30 days."

Why Wix even had a job investigating car thefts was brought into question too. He had served a deputy while his father was Sumner County Sheriff and he got his state job even though he allegedly was behind two other qualified candidates on the civil service list. He also, so claimed some, was put in a pay grade higher than he should have been. His supervisor said she knew he was the son of Representative Wix when she hired Larry, but that he was chosen because of his qualifications alone.

When asked, Representative Wix said he "couldn't remember" if he had spoken to anyone in Governor Lamar Alexander's office about securing the job for his son.

Source:

"Kaplan, Joel. "Gun Incident Brings Rep. Wix's Son Suspension." *The Nashville Tennessean*, April 28, 1983.

A Woman Sues a Drug Company.

On June 12, 1983, Macon County residents Brenda and Lindberg Dennis, filed a federal lawsuit in U.S. District Court against Holland-Rento, Incorporated of Piscataway, New York. The couple asked the court to force Holland-Rento to pay $1 million because of a product the company manufactured that they said caused Brenda permanent injury.

Brenda said that in June 1982, she filled a prescription for a vaginal suppository called "Hyva" at a local pharmacy. Hyva was manufactured by Holland-Rento.

Brenda stated that after using the product once she became "severely ill." Brenda's doctor diagnosed her as suffering from a severe drug reaction and said there was bleeding and damage to Brenda's vaginal area.

Source:

"Law Suit Charges Suppository Use Caused Injury." *The Nashville Tennessean*, June 13, 1983.

A Case of Vehicular Homicide.

On July 1, 1983, Shelby A. Driver, age 31, of Westmoreland faced a preliminary hearing on charges stemming from a truck-car crash on June 10. The wreck resulted in a death, and a home being destroyed by fire. General Sessions Judge Jim Chitwood had appointed Thomas Bilbrey in late June to defend Driver.

The allegations were that on the day of the incident, Driver drove his pickup truck through a four-way stop in Westmoreland and a Tennessee Highway Patrolman gave pursuit. A high-speed chase that reached speeds of up to 80 m.p.h. ensued. The chase ended when Driver either missed a curve or struck another vehicle. Either way, Driver's truck crashed into the home of Jackie Adams. The house caught fire, but Adams escaped the inferno with her children before they were injured.

There were two teenagers riding in the bed of the pickup. One of them was thrown clear of the crash and was uninjured. The other one, Tommy Dwight Wix, age 17, of Portland died at the scene.

A blood alcohol test administered at the scene placed Driver's level at .15 which was well above the limit required to charge him with drunk driving.

Driver was lodged in jail without bond because he was already on parole for a 1980 conviction for grand larceny.

Chitwood bound Driver over to the grand jury that was scheduled to convene on July 18.

Driver was indicted on July 20. He was charged with second-degree murder, vehicular homicide involving alcohol, and vehicular homicide involving reckless driving. District Attorney General Tommy Thompson said a trial jury would decide which of the three charges would apply in the Driver case.

On November 18, 1983, Driver was found guilty of vehicular homicide.

On February 10, 1984, Judge Robert H. Bradshaw held Driver's sentencing hearing. District Attorney General asked for the maximum sentence of 21 years in prison. However, there was some drama to play out before any sentence was rendered.

Before Bradshaw handed down Driver's sentence, he heard a motion from Thomas Bilbrey. Bilbrey motioned that Bradshaw recuse himself from the case. Bilbrey expressed his belief that Judge Bradshaw had both discussed the sentence with District Attorney Thompson and had made up his mind. If biased, of course, Bradshaw could not hand down a fair sentence.

District Attorney Thompson took the stand to contradict Bilbrey's belief. Thompson swore under oath that he had not talked to Bradshaw about the sentencing, and "would not talk to him."

Thompson tried to explain that Bilbrey's belief was based on a misunderstanding. Thompson said that during a conversation with Sumner County detective George Farmer, "I predicted the judge would sentence Driver to 18 or 20 years, and Farmer inferred I had talked with the judge. It was not based on any discussion of the case with the judge because no such discussion ever took place."

After hearing the arguments, Bradshaw ruled that Bilbrey's motion was "without merit" and he sentenced Driver to 16 years in prison.

Bilbrey said he and Driver were disappointed with the sentence and that they were mulling over filing an appeal.

Sources:

Leftwich, J. B. "Judge Won't Quit, Gives Vehicular Homicide Term." *The Nashville Tennessean*, February 11, 1984.

"1 Indicted in Teen's Wreck Death." *The Nashville Tennessean*, July 21, 1983.

"Subject Bound Over On Truck Wreck Charges." *The Nashville Tennessean*, July 2, 1983.

"Vehicular Homicide Hearing Set Today." *The Nashville Tennessean*, July 1, 1983.

A Man Sues an Automaker.

On January 11, 1984, James A. Harris of Lafayette filed suit in Rutherford County Circuit Court accusing the Nissan Motor Manufacturing Corporation of negligence. He said the company was responsible for injuries he received at Nissan truck plant in Smyrna, Tennessee. He asked the court force Nissan to pay him $1 million.

Harris claimed that in January 1983, while working as a pipefitter he was told to install "three jet nozzles" in a large "dip tank" which was filled with a corrosive green liquid. The filing stated that "three days subsequent to immersing his feet and hands into the green liquid substance, his feet cracked or 'busted' open."

Harris also filed a workman's compensation claim against the subcontractor that actually employed him, Hoytt, Brum, and Link, Incorporated of Macon County.

Harris contended that people representing his employer and Nissan told him that the green liquid was harmless. He later learned the substance was a degreaser called "Guanidine" which is known to be a skin irritant.

Harris claimed that he suffered permanent injuries from the degreaser that he was unable to work because of his exposure.

Harris' wife, Teresa, was seeking damages. She asked for an additional $20,000 from Nissan for "loss of income and consortium."

Source:

"Nissan Named in Suit Claiming Work Injuries" *The Nashville Tennessean*, January 12, 1984.

A Foiled Murder Plot.

On January 23, 1984, District Attorney General Tommy Thompson said that a defendant in a kidnapping case was used to help thwart an assassination plot against Thompson. Thompson alleged that the murder plot against him began with a Hartsville businessman. The businessman, never identified by Thompson, wanted revenge over a drug related murder case. Or at least, that's what Thompson thought.

The supposed conspiracy to "hit" Thompson came as a result of the Jeff Cruze case. Cruze, age 24, who was said to be from Lafayette, had admitted guilt in the June 1983 murder of a Florida man identified as a drug dealer. Cruze allegedly worked for the aforementioned Hartsville businessman, but it was never determined concretely that the businessman ordered the hit. Thompson claimed that Cruze even called the businessman while on the run in Florida.

In early January 1984, a person charged with kidnapping whom Thompson was prosecuting, told the district attorney that there was a hit on him. The investigation went quickly and the plot was unraveled easily.

On January 18, 1984, Richard Dale Hesson was charged with solicitation to hire a hitman. However, the businessman Hesson was working on the behalf of was not charged. There was no word as to how Thompson planned to prosecute Hesson without identifying his employer.

Source:

Hampton, Pat. "DA Says His Life Saved from Plot by Informant." *The Nashville Tennessean*, January 24, 1984.

Macon County Sheriff Resigns.

After two years of turmoil, on September 7, 1984, Macon County Sheriff Bill Music resigned. Music's resignation came two days before District Attorney General Tommy Thompson "cleared" him of wrongdoing in the loans and gifts the sheriff's wife took from a prisoner in the Macon County jail. Music admitted that his wife, Faye, accepted loans and gifts amounting to thousands of dollars from convicted felon Brigitte Wilmer. However, Music said the loans were repaid.

Wilmer was serving a term of four years in the Macon County jail after being convicted on a charge of accessory after the fact in the murder of her husband. Faye Music befriended Wilmer and over time the convict loaned the sheriff's wife $4,000 and lavished her with gifts paid for from Wilmer's husband's life insurance policy. There were also statements that Faye Music checked Wilmer out of the jail and drove her to a Nashville shopping mall for shopping sprees paid for by Wilmer.

Bill Music said the investigation into Wilmer "in no means" was the reason he resigned.

For his part, Tommy Thompson said he saw no wrongdoing in Music's actions. Thompson said, "It was more of a judgement problem. As far as I'm concerned, it's over."

Chief Deputy Jerry Gregory was named acting Sheriff until the Macon County Commission named a replacement.

At its next meeting, the Macon County Commission chose between former commissioner, Argo L. "Fats" Browning, and former Chief Deputy James Mercer. The 68-year-old Browning won by a vote of 11 to 9 and he served until the November 6 election when the voters would fill the office.

Eight candidates sought to serve out Music's last two years. They included: Browning, Mercer, Former Sheriff Rex Gann, Red Boiling Springs Chief of Police Scott Brandon, Constable Hillous Dallas, Lonzo Jones, Channey Newberry, and Doyle Brawner.

There was none of the shenanigans that had been alleged in the previous election. Mercer was elected and he served Macon County for many years.

Source:

Blankenship, Harold G. *History of Macon County, Tennessee.* Tompkinsville, Kentucky: Monroe County Press, 1986.

"8 Seek Sheriff's Post in Macon." *The Nashville Tennessean*, September 28, 1984.

"Sheriff Says Loan not Reason for Quitting." *The Nashville Tennessean*, September 10, 1984.

Afterword

It has been tis author's goal for many years to interest more people in their local history before it is lost forever. Thus, I write about things that will stir general interest in the hope that it will lead readers to delve deeper into *their* history. Not only will understanding where they came from give them an appreciation for those that preceded them, but it will also give them a window through which they to look into their future.

Besides that, exploring local history is fun.

About the Author

CL Gammon has had a life-long fascination with the written word. This fascination has led to his authoring more than 70 books.

Over the years, Gammon, who studied Political Science at Tennessee Technological University and History and Government at Hillsdale College, has been the recipient of several prestigious honors and awards. Some of the honors he has received are the Certificate of Appreciation for Service to the State of Tennessee, the Partisan Prohibition Historical Society Citation of Merit (the only two-time recipient), and nomination for the 2023 Gilder Lehrman Lincoln Prize.

Several universities, including the State University of New York, the University of Akron, and East Mississippi Community College, have utilized his books as course material.

Articles written by Gammon have appeared in more than a dozen national and regional publications. He has also written feature articles for his hometown newspaper, *The Macon County Times*.

CL Gammon lives in Lafayette, Tennessee.

www.ingramcontent.com/pod-product-compliance
Lightning Source LLC
Chambersburg PA
CBHW060357050426
42449CB00009B/1773